THE SECRETS OF BUY TO LET SUCCESS

TO LET SUCCESS

EXPERT TIPS ON HOW TO MAKE
MONEY FROM PROPERTY

By Nick Fox

ISBN: 978-0-9927817-2-9

First published in England in 2014 by Fox Print Partners

THE SECRETS OF BUY TO LET SUCCESS

EXPERT TIPS ON HOW TO MAKE MONEY FROM PROPERTY

by Nick Fox

with Sarah Walker

published by Fox Print Partners

Contents

About the Author   8

Author's disclaimer   12

Foreword   14

PART ONE:
WHERE DO YOU START AS A
PROPERTY INVESTOR?   17

Chapter 1   Before Investing   18
Chapter 2   Timing   27
Chapter 3   Raising Finance   46
Chapter 4   Finding A Property   63
Chapter 5   How And Where To Find A Bargain   75
Chapter 6   Types of Investment Property   85

PART TWO:
MAKING MONEY FROM PROPERTY   101

Chapter 7   Generating An Income   102
Chapter 8   Letting Your Property   115
Chapter 9   Investing Overseas   127

PART THREE:
MANAGING YOUR INVESTMENT PROPERTY   133

Chapter 10   Being A Landlord   134
Chapter 11   A Landlord's Responsibilities   149
Chapter 12   Tax And Property Investment   153

PART FOUR:
CONSOLIDATION   163

Chapter 13   Portfolio Building   164
Chapter 14   Your Exit Strategy   173

Summary   177

Amazon reviews for HMO Property Success   183

Testimonials   186

For my family, friends and business partners.
You all inspire me daily.
Thank you.

About the Author

At an age when most children are busy worrying about what and how many sweets their parents are going to buy them, Nick took matters into his own hands.

"When I was eight, I realised that if you really want something, you need to find a way to get it and there is always a way, even if it's just a packet of sweets.

So instead of waiting and saving up my pocket money I decided to invest the little bit I had. I bought up all the one penny sweets from the scout tuck shop and sold them to my friends for 2p.

That was a quite a return on investment."

In those early days, what Nick lacked in terms of money he more than made up for in his desire to turn what he had into something much bigger – 100% bigger in this case!

From this early success, he developed an entrepreneurial mindset, which helped Nick grow a technology business from scratch to a million pound enterprise, before he went on to apply those same principles successfully to property investment.

No entrepreneur's life story would be complete without a disaster or two along the way. Nick's life started out ordinarily enough. He lived in a static home with his mother and had a happy childhood, apart from one day he still looks back on as a major turning point in his life: the day his family home burnt down.

That was a watershed. He and his mother had lost everything without any warning. Luckily, the insurance money they received for the damage helped them to buy a house, which also happened to be a complete wreck. This would become Nick's first exposure to a path familiar to most buy to let investors, i.e. find a property, do it up and either sell it or rent it out for a profit.

From the ashes of their home, Nick and his mother embarked on a journey that would see them buy several houses, knock them into shape and sell them on for a profit. They continued to do this until they had made enough money to buy Nick's mother her dream house. The lessons Nick learned from the experience stayed with him and have proved very useful in his life as a property investor.

Prior to moving into property full time, Nick had already demonstrated a knack for seeing where the next big opportunities were and going after them. He was self-employed from the age of 18, selling software to some small independent retailers. Software in the late 80s and 90s was one of the fastest growing business sectors and he was soon distributing more than a million units of that software into Dixons, Woolworths and WHSmiths. But by the time the mid-2000s came, he was already looking for the next big project. This time it was back to the passion of his youth - property investment.

"The 1990s was a time of great changes. Computers and software were advancing rapidly as we went from very basic computers to highly sophisticated machines and the growth of search engines. It was an exciting time.

The idea of being a full time buy to let investor only really took off in the mid -1990s but it has always been a fantastic way to make money – if you take the long-term view and buy wisely. My only regret is that I didn't join the boom in buy to let investment sooner."

Nick had bought his first property in 1986, at the age of 18, but before jumping into property investment full time, he read every property book and visited every property website he could find to gain insight into the world of property from an investor's point of view. And then he got stuck in.

Since the early 2000s Nick has been building a portfolio that currently numbers over 200 properties and he has no intentions of stopping there. He now has a team of people who help him manage this portfolio so that he can go and do the other things in life that keep him balanced.

"It's important to have balance in your life. Having other things to think about can really help you, whether you are busy growing a property portfolio or any other kind of business. You must make time for your family and help others along the way."

Nick is a keen supporter of various charities and a patron of Peace One Day.

Author's disclaimer

I am not qualified to give financial or legal advice. All related recommendations made in this book should only be considered in consultation with suitably qualified and accredited professionals. Persons giving financial advice MUST be properly qualified and regulated by the Financial Services Authority (FSA) and anyone giving you legal advice should be suitably qualified and regulated by The Law Society and the Solicitors Regulation Authority (SRA) (or the Council of Licensed Conveyancers (CLC)).

Also by Nick Fox:

HMO Property Success

Property Investment Success

Foreword

How many buy to let property investors do you know?

Buy to let was once the preserve of the wealthy few, but in the last 20 years people from all walks of life have become property investors, from your neighbours to your friends – maybe even your parents! Everyone knows a property investor somewhere.

If buy to let is a national pastime, then house prices have become the national obsession. Whether you've been having a quiet afternoon drink at the pub or just bumping into some parents on the school run, the chances are you'll have ended up talking about house prices at some point.

When house prices are going up everyone gets excited; when they're spiralling downwards the national mood sinks with them. There has rarely been a worse period for national sentiment than the great house price collapse of 2008. This was the year when the dream of property prices rising forever died across the UK.

Like all of the lessons you learn in life, 2008 taught us a very valuable one. Property is an investment like any other: prices will rise but they will fall as well. If you own a house, you can't simply use it as a cash machine.

Anyone who becomes a property investor realises this fundamental truth at some point – hopefully sooner, rather than later! - and this lies at the heart of the advantages you will eventually gain on your journey to financial freedom and a retirement free from money worries.

This book is about teaching you the basics of property investment, so that you can take each step one at a time. It doesn't come with a guarantee that you'll become a property millionaire, but what it will show you is the process and the things you need to consider.

My aims with this book are to:

- Help you understand the property investment market
- Make you aware of financing options and how much money you need
- Help you identify the right kind of investment properties
- Show you how to manage your buy to let business

And, of course, explain how to make a profit on your investment!

"My interest is in the future because I am going to spend the rest of my life there."

Charles Kettering, Social Philosopher

PART ONE:

WHERE DO YOU START AS A PROPERTY INVESTOR?

Chapter 1

Before Investing

Why invest in property?

The answer to this should be, why not? You can choose to put your money in a lot of places, depending on your appetite for risk. One place might be in a tin under the bed or you could, like most people, put it in a savings account. You could invest it in stocks and shares or even a start up a business.

So let's take a closer look at these alternatives before we move on to property.

If you opt to keep all your money in a tin under the bed to protect it, you'll find that something very strange begins to happen to that money. It starts to disappear.

I'm not suggesting that someone is opening up your tin of cash and dipping into it now and again. The money disappears without you even opening this tin. This is because of inflation, which raises the cost of living over time. Something that cost you £100 in 1984 would cost you around £300 today. The longer you keep your cash without doing anything with it, the more it will lose its value.

This leaves us with our second option: a high street bank savings account.

This is the option most people take with their money. Haven't we all been brought up to see the bank as the safest place to store our cash? This faith has only been seriously tested once in most people's lifetimes, and that was in 2008, when we all got a reality check:

Money in the bank is not necessarily ours when it comes to the crunch!

I'm not going to tell you <u>not</u> to keep your money in the bank or in a tin under the bed because sometimes these may be the best options you have. It is always wise to keep some money by for a rainy day and the bank is probably the best place for it in those cases. Yet even there your money will lose its value over time and, again, that's down to inflation.

Inflation loves to eat your money. The long-term average inflation rate in the UK, based on the everyday things you buy is 5.58%. The best interest rate the bank will give you (even on an ISA) when I last checked in 2014 was about 1.5%.

The stark choice, then, is between losing the full 5.58% of your money over a lifetime or losing an average 4.08% every year (assuming the banks don't suddenly decide to become more generous). So how do you stop your money disappearing?

The answer is to invest money. This can be in a business, stocks and shares or an asset of some kind – such as property.

If you invest money in a business there is always risk. There is a risk that the business will fail and the reality is that most start-ups do fail in the first 5 years. That risk is there, even if you invest in an established business. Look at what happened to Comet, Woolworths, HMV and other high street names we always took for granted, as established 'big' businesses. They have all disappeared, only to be replaced by derelict units with apologetic signs thanking everyone for their custom.

You can't live in a business and it won't put a roof over your head if the cash flow runs dry.

Why property is less risky

The great thing about property is that no matter how much money you put into it, over time you will almost certainly get a return on that investment. It might take years or it could take as little as a month, depending on what property you buy, where you buy it and, just as importantly, when.

People can manage without money, they can choose where to shop and do business but they can't manage without shelter. Everyone needs somewhere to live and the population in most countries is rising. In cities such as London, the supply of property is under severe strain. Foreign investors and city dwellers are prepared to battle it out for available properties, which inevitably pushes up prices.

Simple supply and demand will continue to raise property prices in the long term, regardless of recessions or economic crises. Investing in property for the long term will protect you from the effects of the economic 'troughs' that inevitably come with the 'peaks', and can give you the level of financial freedom you desire.

What remains something of an unknown is exactly when and by how much prices will fluctuate. Most property agents and sales people will tell you that property doubles in value every ten years. I can confidently put that myth to bed now: it doesn't, at least not always and not in every area. Like any investment, the value can go down as well as up, even if the long-term trend is one of increasing value.

Fortunately, the capital value of property rising is by no means the only reason that buy to let can be such a safe and lucrative long term investment. And that's what I'm going to show you in this book.

What kind of property investor are you?

All property investors are the same, aren't they? No. Property investors can come from all walks of life. Some will be part-time investors who hold down a day job while pursuing their investment dreams in the few hours they get outside of work. Some will be professional investors who devote their lives to property investment and make a fortune. Others will fall somewhere in between.

Success in property can mean different things to different people, however if you define success as having a million-pound property portfolio, then the distinctions between investor types become more important.

What type of investor are you?

Do you have the right approach that will allow you to reach your goal?

I've met many different kinds of investor over the years - some sophisticated, some downright reckless and others at the point of 'guru' status. Here are some of those people:

Richard – The Adventurous Investor

Richard is the suave, casual kind of property investor who has money and a licence to spend it. He wears his suit loose with no tie and has no care for conventions. It's his way or the highway and to hell with the details.

Money is no real object to Richard - he has plenty. Richard likes to take risks because it's all about the adrenaline and the thrill of the chase for him. Property investment is a gamble and it doesn't matter if that property is in Albania or Blackburn; if there is a deal to be done you'll find Richard entering the market first, before anyone else.

Richard relies on luck more than judgement and it sometimes pays off. But then that luck runs out or he misses some of the detail in a rental return that sounded too good to be true...and was.

Being an adventurous investor can be seen as reckless and relies on you having enough money not to worry about your losses when a property market goes bad. It also requires a lot of self belief and resilience, to be able to put mistakes in the past and move on to the next big market and that next potential windfall.

Richard's approach is all about short-term gain, which is definitely not a strategy for the faint hearted.

Suzanne – The Experienced Investor
Suzanne has been in the property business for more than a decade now. In that time she has built up a substantial portfolio of properties that have allowed her to spread her risk. She focuses more on ongoing rental returns than on any short-term gains to be made.

Suzanne will study an area and go through every detail about a property before making the decision to invest. She will look to buy at a knockdown price, or unearth a hidden gem in a sought-after area of town that just needs some refurbishment work to realise its potential. She will have a good relationship with a number of estate agents who find her the right properties that will expand her portfolio.

Before choosing her property, Suzanne will look closely at all the details, from location to the likely rental return. She rarely acts on impulse and won't take risks unless they are calculated carefully beforehand.

Julian – The Analytical Investor
Julian is like Suzanne in some ways – until he has to make a decision. He is known for overanalysing every situation, often held back by the sheer amount of knowledge he has about property investment.

Julian has read every book, visited every Internet blog and attended his fair share of property shows over the years. The one thing he hasn't done is move beyond his one investment property.

This is because he knows that property markets move in cycles and by the time he feels comfortable that the next up-cycle has arrived, he is already listening to the news and worrying about when the end of it will come.

Julian is afflicted by what some people in the property game call 'analysis paralysis'. He simply doesn't move quickly enough and won't take any risks because his knowledge about the subject gets in the way. And so he misses out time and again on good, solid investment opportunities simply because he's waiting for 'the perfect deal'.

Graham – The Novice Investor

Graham works full time as an engineer and has his pet project. The converted old church he has been working on for three years is beginning to look the part but there is still a lot of work to do. His ambition is to finish the project in a year or two and move on to another house.

The property is large and in an up and coming location, so he expects it to generate a good income in time and provide him with a nest egg for retirement. The only problem is Graham hasn't set a goal for when the project will actually be finished.

The house means a lot to him so he has become emotionally attached and there is no real plan in place to address what happens when the property is finished. Will it be sold or rented out? Has all the investment been worth it?

Why buy to let investors need to be good all-rounders

Each of these investor types has a different motivation for becoming involved in buy to let property. What you can learn from their profiles is that becoming a successful property investor will require a number of skills.

You'll need to be able to separate your emotions from each project and have the ability to take a calculated risk. You will be more successful if you're prepared to work at it, rather than expecting the right investments to simply fall into your lap. Trust me they won't; investing and being a success in property takes work and organisation. And you need to be clear on why you're investing, so that you can put together an investment profile that will help you achieve your financial goals.

Property is a risk like any other investment. It's only by taking a long-term view and having a well-considered plan, that those risks can be reduced.

Chapter 2

Timing

When is it a good time to invest in property?

One of the most common questions I get asked is, when is the right time to invest in property? Well, if you've explored all the other investment options available, compared the likely returns on offer and are convinced that property is the right investment for you, then you don't actually need to ask this question.

It's bit like asking when should I start my weight loss programme or when should I start running to get myself fit? Investing in property shouldn't be something you put in a calendar and say, "I'll start doing it next month / next year". Once you've decided on property and have the means and time available to do it, the time to start investing is now. If you don't make your move now then you're only reducing the potential gains you can make.

If your aim is to make enough money to generate a decent retirement income, then you will need to have invested in property for at least 10 years.

Obviously, your age will be a factor guiding your investment decisions because running a portfolio of investments at 80 years old plus won't be much fun. If your goal is to retire early you're likely to need more than one buy to let property and you will want to be in a position to relax a bit by then.

The great thing about property investment is that no matter when you decide to do it, there is never a wrong time to invest. As you become more experienced, you'll be able to identify better times to invest to maximise your returns, but there are always good deals to be done.

Your ability to look at the economic climate you're in and see how this is affecting the attitudes of both buyers and sellers will have a major impact on how successful you can be in the long term. In theory – the sky is the limit!

At the moment, we're in a climate of growing optimism.

Unemployment is falling, house prices are rising again and there are Government measures in place to help people climb onto the property ladder. Even the banks are more sympathetic if you ask them for a mortgage.

Although the recent introduction of new measures to ensure responsible lending means a more rigorous application process, 95 % loan to value mortgages, unthinkable a few years ago, are now being routinely handed out (with Government help) to homebuyers with decent credit ratings.

As for landlords, most have enjoyed a long period of strong rental growth and low voids while people were hard pressed to buy their homes. Even if they bought prior to the housing market crash, then the money they have made from rent and the increased capital growth they are likely to be seeing now will have more than compensated for any temporary drop in value. And there needn't be much worry about the demand for rental properties dropping because although more people are coming into the buying market, there is still a huge lack of supply for those still looking to rent.

The one thing you may notice is that the window of opportunity is starting to close on the bargains you may have found in the down cycle, but there is still time to find them. Remember, property investment should always be viewed as a long-term investment rather than a get rich quick scheme – I've yet to find one of those that actually works!

The property market cycle
One of the first things you should be familiar with if you want to get the best out of buy to let is the investment cycle.

Property, as we have established, is an investment. If you happen to already deal with stocks and shares you'll be familiar with an investment cycle, but if you're new to investing you need to make sure you understand this.

What is an investment cycle?

An investment cycle helps investors identify where a market is at. Imagine a clock face for a moment, with the market peak at 12 o'clock and the market hitting bottom at 6 o'clock. In between these two extremes you will have lots of other things happening that will cause property prices to either rise or fall. Notice I said rise *or fall*? Property prices are always moving in one direction or another!

If you look hard enough, there will always be certain indicators that will help you decide on the best times to buy for high capital growth or strong rental yields. The evidence will be obvious as long as you have the ability to read the signals.

These signals can be extremely valuable and you'll come across them from time to time whether you're watching the TV or out having a drink with friends. I remember one occasion when a friend living in Manchester said to me, "I've noticed some big changes lately. It's easy to get hold of builders and even the plumber turns up on time. Normally when I call them I get an answer machine and they don't return my call."

Is the builder returning your calls?

So why is it that builders are sometimes more eager to return your calls? The answer is a quiet property market or one that has reached the bottom of its cycle. Builders are only busy when there is a profit to be made from building or renovating houses.

So, naturally, when demand is falling, there is less major building work going on. Builders are now having to go out and find work and this makes them more eager to take your calls and book in your jobs, no matter how small.

That's an example of a fairly subtle sign. Perhaps the most telling signal you'll get is from the people who work at the sharp end of the property market – the estate agents. The life of an estate agent is rarely straightforward. There's always uncertainty around every corner, whether or not the investment cycle is moving up or down.

If you have ever tried to sell your house at the bottom of the investment cycle, you'll notice that the agent will take their time returning your calls. This is because they will have more properties than interested buyers. From an investment perspective, if the agents already have lots of properties on their books, it's a buyer's market and a good time to make your move. There should be a lot of sellers prepared to make a good deal and you should be able to buy something with 'built in equity' ready for the start of the next market cycle.

The giveaway clues that a property market is reaching a peak
One telling clue that the property market cycle is about to pass its peak is when the media starts to report the kind of news that sends shockwaves around the world, such as a break-up of the Eurozone or wars.

This kind of news can spread negative sentiment even in previously fast-growing property markets. As I've already mentioned, you must remember that a property market, like any other investment market, is dynamic. It can go in all sorts of directions but it never stands still.

Anything that creates financial uncertainty usually impacts the property market, as people don't want to make big financial decisions when they're not sure how things are likely to look in the near future.

It can be an emotional reason or perception that affects how people behave over property, or it can be a real financial and economic reason. They call can and will keep happening periodically - the important thing is not to worry about fluctuations. When the market has passed the peak of its cycle, this is just part of the rebalancing that will always take place. And when everyone is running for cover because they fear the end of the world, this is usually the best time to invest!

What happens at the bottom of a cycle?

When a property market reaches the bottom of its cycle, you have a 'buyers' market'. The bottom of the market is a thoroughly depressing time for most of the population but not if you're an investor. When things get really bad and everyone is fed up, this is usually the best time to invest.

The bottom of the property cycle tends to coincide with a national economy that is in recession, negative wage growth, job losses and pessimism about the future. This is the time when people are more likely to be forced into selling property.

You also get a period of low or unstable interest rates. As we have recently witnessed, governments will step in to soften the blow by cutting interest rates, which brings mortgage payments down. Unfortunately, as those mortgage payments are coming down, so is the price of property for many homeowners and this is when negative equity will rear its ugly head.

There is one section of the population who will be having a much better time at this point - buy to let investors! You can now make the kinds of offers on property that would have been laughed off months earlier. I would say that this is actually the best time to invest in property.

Sellers will soon be panicking and dropping their asking prices further and if you time it right, you can reap the rewards of rising prices in the long term. You certainly won't have much competition either. At these times, even some investors will be opting to wait and see.

This is also the stage when rental returns will rise as people put off buying houses until the market recovers and demand for lettings will be high.

What happens when a property market is in recovery?

The recovery is when everyone starts feeling good about property again. When the property cycle moves into a recovery phase, selling houses starts to get easier. As prices begin to rise along with demand, the number of people you see looking for homes increases. More buyers will enter the market supported by better mortgage lending conditions and buyer incentives.

The oversupply of properties we saw at the bottom of the market will soon be absorbed as the recovery gathers pace. Many smaller developers and construction companies will have been forced out of business and projects mothballed, adding to the pressure on the supply.

Landlords can still benefit from rising rents during the recovery as supply struggles to keep up with demand. Statistics will alert the banks that asking prices are increasing in some areas and they will have little choice other than to increase their valuations as a result.

Soon you get a property boom where prices start rising by double digits on an annual basis and this can last for several years. It usually slows again when construction levels are at a point where supply becomes more balanced with demand.

At this point, media hype will add more fuel to the boom, convincing people to buy before property prices rise again. Property prices can literally rise in a week. It's not unusual for offers to be made and accepted on the spot, making it almost impossible to negotiate a good deal. Why should an owner take your offer when there are plenty more people willing to pay the full asking price?

What happens at the peak of the investment cycle?

When the property market is at its peak, sellers are now firmly in the driving seat. If you have a portfolio and are considering an exit from your investment, the peak of the cycle may be your best window of opportunity to sell. The owner of a property can dictate all the terms. They will be unwilling to negotiate on anything, including price – unless they are in a desperate hurry to sell.

The peak of the market means that affordability will be hitting a peak as well. At this point, the property cycle is about to move into freefall as people start to see property as too expensive and/or find it unaffordable. Those already in property decide to sit tight for the moment and first time buyers or perhaps those between homes decide to become tenants instead, as they can rent a better home than they can buy, while continuing to save a bigger deposit.

At the peak of the cycle, housing developers will still be bringing more properties onto the market. We've seen this happening in recent years with flats, where a flood of new builds at the peak of the market has saturated it, and towns and cities start to have properties standing unsold for months or even years. This glut of stock starts to result in an increase in repossessions as the value of property quickly falls and the banks start getting nervous about mortgages.

The big housing developers who have relied so much on demand being maintained suddenly find that their sales forecasts are way off the mark. The banks, sensing that all is not well, begin to question those forecasts. New properties are soon discounted, which has a knock-on effect on the rest of the market.

As the investment cycle comes full circle and arrives again at the bottom, this will be the time to look for those bargain properties once again.

TIP: *The best time to pick up bargains is at the bottom of the investment cycle, when demand is low and you can negotiate hard.*

What did we learn from the market crash?

2008 is often cited as the year when the credit crunch began, but things were going wrong much earlier than that. The credit crunch was something very few people believed would really happen and most felt like they had sleepwalked right into it.

That's the thing with ground-shaking events in history; you often don't feel them until they have already been and gone.

The housing market crash that hit the UK in the winter of 2007 could be seen as part of the fall out of the sub-prime mortgage crisis that had gripped the US the previous summer. Sure enough, the ripples of that disaster were hitting the shores of the UK, even before the full effect was felt on house prices.

But it was actually a year earlier that a nervous UK Government started to wonder just how long the housing boom would continue. Was this the first time in history that house prices would just keep rising?

And house prices were rising fast in 2006 – by more than 10% every 12 months. At this time you could have bought and sold a modest 2-bedroom terrace almost anywhere and doubled your money inside five years.

This consistently fast price growth was a matter of growing concern with the Bank of England. So they duly began raising interest rates and did it not once, but five times between August 2006 and August 2007.

Little did they know that the catastrophic financial crisis that was gripping the US at the time would soon become global and the biggest single collapse since the Great Depression of 1929.

So, with house prices starting to tumble throughout the UK in 2008 (apart from a few outposts in Scotland) the situation and outlook was a grim one for both investors and homeowners, who had both grown used to easy credit and easy profit.

Suddenly, investors who had over-leveraged themselves with 'no money down' investments found that the whole stack of cards was about to collapse on top of them. Many went bankrupt and many companies that had made millions on the back of property investors hungry for 'easy money' began to fold in dramatic fashion.

Harsh lessons were learned, we all realised that there really is no 'sure thing' in investment. The property boom had wiped out memories of negative equity and the times when more than 30% was wiped off the value of homes in the early 1990s. This boom was different – or so everyone thought.

If anything good came out of the crash of 2007-08, it was the realisation that houses cannot be used as cash machines. Just as money doesn't grow on trees, property values can come crashing to earth with a bang.

If you want to make money within this cyclic market and succeed in buy to let, one of the most important rules to follow is to invest in property that not only cover its own costs, but also operate at a profit.

If your rental income isn't covering your mortgage payments and running costs and you end up in a down cycle, it can take a very long time to recover. You can't rely on the value of property to rise in the short term, so you must plan to achieve consistent returns from rental profit, while you wait for the capital value to rise over the long term.

Property investment myths

I still have several books, written by property investment 'gurus', who poured cold water on the idea that a housing market crash was on the horizon. Instead, they preferred to keep selling the 'secrets' of property investment based on capital increases to others who thought house prices would never fall.

With hindsight, it's easy to look back and laugh at the misguided predictions of those who should have seen what was coming. Some did - there were also property experts who predicted the 2008 crash as early as 2005.

Not surprisingly, you don't hear much from the 'no money down, build a million-pound portfolio' gurus any more. Rather, those investors who understood how investment cycles work are the ones who continued to profit throughout the crash and are still around. They will have bought in the early part of the last decade, from 2001 onwards, and reaped the benefits of a buy and hold strategy. They were the tortoises rather than the hares. And in property it's always better to be the tortoise because what goes around comes around, eventually.

Myths are a powerful thing. We all like to hear them, whether they're good or bad. It's human nature to collectively fall in line with myths that are put out there to scare us or persuade us into making certain decisions. But blindly believing myths often leads us to make the wrong decisions and miss opportunities. Here are three big myths that you often hear about the property market:

Myth 1: Property is overvalued

I picked up the Daily Mail newspaper one morning as I was writing this book and saw a headline that pretty much sums up why people continue to be cautious about investing in property – even in a growing market.

It read:

'House Prices To Soar Until 2020!'

'Middle Income Earners Will Be Priced Out!'

The myth you will see crop up again and again is the price to earnings ratio. This is the price of property compared to the income of the average working person. The logic goes that the higher property prices rise, the more out of reach houses become for the average person and people then see property as becoming overvalued.

So why then were property price to income ratios more than 4 ½ times the average salary in 2004? People were still buying property and continued to do so in enough numbers to sustain a house price boom that lasted until outside events ended it in 2007.

The answer to this is mortgages. Whether you're a buy to let investor or a homebuyer, unless you're lucky, you will be relying on the bank to give you a mortgage. The amount of interest you pay on that mortgage and on what terms is the most important driver of a property market.

If people have the means to buy property and the bank is confident enough to lend that money, then they will buy.

For example:

Mr Stevens invests in a property.
He borrows £100,000 and his annual mortgage interest payment is 10%.
The interest costs him £100,000 x 10% = £10,000 a year.

Then the banks and lenders lower interest rates.

Mr Stevens invests in a larger property, borrowing £200,000 and his mortgage interest is 5%
The interest costs him £200,000 x 5% = £10,000 a year.

The mortgage borrowing has doubled, even though his costs are the same.

In recent years we have seen a historically low interest rate environment. Those investors who are able to lock in low interest rates on their mortgages will benefit from lower monthly payments. So the price to income ratio argument fails to stack up.

Myth 2: Property prices will take decades to recover
This is one of my favourite examples. It's the kind of myth you might hear people talking about down at the pub. Anyone who is struggling to sell their property will latch on to this myth, even though historically there has and always will be cause for optimism.

A case in point was Florida in the USA. House prices were predicted never to recover as recently as 2010, such was the impact of the sub-prime crisis. But as soon as the banks started lending again, people started buying again. Some of the worst-affected cities in Florida between 2007 and 2009 are now seeing property prices rising by more than 20% a year!

It would take a catastrophe of global proportions to alter a long-term trend of rising prices, and that's been the case for as long as anyone can remember. This is a key factor in making property such a great investment.

Myth 3: Property prices and rents are rising

When I hear anyone say that property prices and rents are rising – at the same time and at the same rate - I immediately smell a rat.

The reason? As we've established, property markets move in cycles. When prices are falling, it generally means people have stopped buying because they are unable to get a mortgage. This is when we see a surge in rents.

Post-2008 in the UK saw 7% per annum rises in rents, as people who should have been first-time property buyers found it almost impossible to get a mortgage.

In areas where property is in demand, rents naturally rise when the average person is not in a position to buy. This is why buy to let investors were able to capitalise on a rental bonanza as most of the country was struggling through a recession.

During a recovery, which, let's face it, is usually supported by a boom in house prices, people are out there buying again. When people can buy, armed with Government incentives such as Help

To Buy, they are less likely to want to rent. In this case, rental growth begins to slow.

This explains why you're unlikely to see rising prices and rising rents at the same time.

The good thing from an investment point of view is:

Whatever the economy is doing, you can still make money.

"The best time to plant a tree was 20 years ago. The second best time is now."

Chinese Proverb

Chapter 3

Raising Finance

You don't need to be wealthy to be a property investor, but it helps!

That doesn't mean that it's impossible to make money in property if you're not wealthy; the trick is to find a way to get your hands on some financing. In terms of your own cash contribution, this may be earnings from your job, profits from a business venture or the savings you have built up and put by over the years. You could even re-mortgage your home if you have enough equity in it.

Another possibility is to raise finance via a commercial mortgage - either a business mortgage or a commercial investment mortgage. If your business is doing well and has a strong credit rating then this might be an ideal route because it could offer more protection than taking a risk by putting your home up as security on a loan. High street banks will typically offer 50% LTV mortgages while some specialist lenders might be prepared to raise that LTV to 75%.

TIP: *Invest only what you can afford to lose!*

Nobody wants to think about losing money. Even so, the amount you decide to invest should be an amount you can afford to lose if things go wrong. To be a successful property investor, you will need to take a calculated risk, but there is no cast-iron guarantee that the risk will pay off – and that's something we'll cover later in this book.

The price of an average house in a reasonable area in the UK is about £170,000 at the time of writing. Any less than this and either the property will be in a very poor state of repair or the area you're investing in clearly isn't very popular with people looking to rent or buy - which rather defeats the purpose!

This isn't to say you can't make money buying cheaper properties. Bargains do exist and there are always opportunities to buy a wreck and fix it up. If you go down this route you will really need to know what you're doing as buying cheap is never a guarantee of investment success.

So when you decide to invest in your first property, there is a good chance that you'll need to go to the bank to raise some financing in the form of a buy to let mortgage. You'll find hundreds of different products out there offered by lenders. As a rule of thumb, be prepared to have to put up at least 15% of the value of the property yourself as a deposit.

Although this mortgage will primarily be granted on the basis of the rental income stacking up, the banks still expect you as a buy to let investor to already have some investment money available – it gives them additional confidence that you are a risk worth taking.

If you happen to be a cash buyer, then this opens up a whole range of possibilities that will not be available to those needing finance. As well as the obvious advantage of being able to negotiate hard with vendors who need a quick sale, you'll also be able to use the money to buy at auction and not have to wait for clearance of funds from the bank.

TIP: *Beware of using a mortgage to buy at auction!*

The biggest risk with using a mortgage to fund the purchase of an auction property is that you may end up seriously out of pocket if your mortgage doesn't clear on time. On the day of the auction you must lodge a 10% deposit and the contracts are signed then and there, i.e. you are legally committed to the purchase. You usually then have just 28 days to complete, so if there is a problem or delay with your mortgage application and you can't complete, there will be financial penalties, including losing your deposit, and you may lose the property as well.

Another option – and this is only something you should tackle if you already have an investment track record and a clear business plan – is to do a joint venture with someone. They can provide the money and you provide the know-how and your time, or you can both put in some of each. The arrangement needs to be set out legally, but it's certainly an option and something I've done myself in expanding and diversifying my portfolio.

In short, there is nearly always a way to raise finance, you just need to have focus and a realistic plan to get there.

How much money do you need?

It might sound like I'm stating the obvious, but it's really important you understand how much money you need in order to be able to invest. I've lost count of the number of people I've met who tell me they really want to 'get into property' but that they only have a small amount of savings and they don't think they can get much via mortgage finance. There still seems to be a perception out there that you can get something for nothing with property investment!

If you only have £10,000 to invest yourself, you're not going to be able to buy much in the UK, especially when you consider all the other things you need to pay for.

It's easy to focus purely on the property itself and ignore the other associated costs, which can really mount up. That being said, those added costs still look small compared to the £150,000 or so you will have to invest in the actual bricks and mortar (via deposit and mortgage).

Some of the costs you need to consider are:

- ○ Stamp duty
- ○ Solicitor's fees
- ○ Survey
- ○ Refurbishment and maintenance work
- ○ Management fees
- ○ Letting agent fees

...to name but a few.

You'll need to set aside funds for all of the above, which can run into thousands of pounds. You should work these costs into your financial plan to make sure the investment pays for itself, but you must be able to cover them, personally, if something goes wrong with your buy to let. And it doesn't stop there.

You will also need to cover any potential void periods – the term for those times where you can't find a tenant and the property stands empty.

If you own the property outright, voids will not be as much of an issue, but if your mortgage payments are covered by the rental income then you should budget for having at least 3 months' worth of emergency money set aside to cover these periods.

Let's look at the following example to help illustrate how much money you might need to finance your investment.

- Mr and Mrs Andrews hope to purchase a property for £150,000
- They manage to secure a mortgage for £120,000 (80% LTV)
- They invest £30,000 as a deposit

Now, if Mr and Mrs Andrews are just starting out, they're unlikely to buy a new property as their first investment, so they will have set aside some money to cover costs.

- 15% to cover refurbishment and any maintenance
- 5% to cover any void periods when the property is ready to rent.

This comes to a total of £30,000 extra they will need to set aside, in addition to the deposit, to make a life a bit more comfortable, and that's not including the initial purchase costs, for which they will need to budget around 2% of the purchase price, £3,000. (This percentage rises accordingly with the stamp duty thresholds.)

There are of course a number of ways to raise this additional money, although it's best if you already have the funds yourself. You could secure a bank loan, but that will set you back a lot in interest payments, depending on the term of the loan and the interest rate. You could also, as mentioned above, do a joint venture with someone who has money to invest but is short on time and expertise.

TIP: *Whatever route you take, you must make sure your borrowing doesn't leave you overexposed!*

Plan and budget carefully, or you run the risk of killing any property portfolio ambitions before they get started.

Getting finance

Right now is a fantastic time to start thinking about investing in property. In fact, the best times to start thinking about investing are those times when it costs less to borrow money. Interest rates have been at historic lows since 2008, when the Bank of England Base Rate was reduced dramatically to try and stimulate the UK economy.

The Bank of England uses the powerful weapon of interest rates to control the economy. If economic growth is racing away then the chances are you'll see the Base Rate increased to control inflation. When the economic numbers are looking shaky, for example, unemployment is rising and GDP grinds to a halt or goes into the negative, then the Base Rate is reduced.

Whether it's rising or falling, the Base Rate is closely tracked by the banks, who set their own interest rates to follow suit. So if unemployment drops to a certain level, then the Bank of England policy committee may decide it's a good time to raise the rate. And if they do, then mortgages become more expensive.

And the potential highs and lows cover quite a broad spectrum. You may or may not remember mortgage interest rates running at 15% back in the early 1990s. That's in stark contrast to the 3% to 5% you can typically get today.

As I explained earlier, there are many ways to get finance. If you decide on a high street bank or building society then you will need to go through a long process of finding a bank willing to lend you the money and making sure that all your finances are in order.

A buy to let mortgage quote can be done over the phone with a few simple questions, but the process really starts when you need to produce the following:

- Proof of income
- Proof of the source of your deposit
- Details of your experience as a landlord
- A surveyor's valuation of the rental amount

While banks have become slightly more willing to lend money now that the property market is improving, you will still need a clean credit rating and be in a position to provide evidence of the above.

The good news for you as an investor is that buy to let mortgages don't currently fall under the scope of the Financial Services Authority, and therefore you won't be affected by the new, more stringent checks that have been introduced for primary residence mortgages.

For these applications for a mortgage to buy your own home, you'll need to provide much more detailed proof of income, savings, investments and pensions. The banks' scoring systems also now look at things like regular payments going out of your bank account and your lifestyle, in order to assess your financial commitments in much more detail than they used to. All this is to assess how risky you are to lend to and you should be prepared for at least two or three visits to the bank or some lengthy phone calls. You'll need to shop around to get the best deal and you may face rejection from some lenders.

However, as a buy to let investor, the main thing the bank is interested in is the potential rental income being high enough to cover the monthly mortgage repayments. Currently, most lenders ask for proof (from a surveyor) that the rental income covers at least 125% of the proposed repayment amount. Your personal financial situation and your experience as a landlord come second to that, and are really more to ensure you are a credible person to lend to.

Even though buy to let mortgage applications are far less onerous than primary residence ones, I'd still advise you to engage a mortgage broker or independent financial advisor (IFA) to do all this for you. As you become a more experienced property investor, a good mortgage broker will be an important part of your investment team and I'll go into more detail later in this chapter.

What you need to know about buy to let mortgages

One of the most important things to understand about a buy to let mortgage is that you cannot use it to finance a property you intend to live in.

This is because the bank has assessed your buy to let mortgage using a different set of criteria than your standard mortgage, as mentioned in the last section. The latter is assessed purely on your income and your ability to pay back the loan over 25 years or so. A buy to let mortgage will be based on the income you can make from renting out the property.

Another crucial difference between the two mortgages is the loan to value or the deposit you need to put in. In the heady days prior to 2007 it was possible to get 100% or more, such was the confidence among the banks. The financial crisis changed all that, yet even now, with schemes such as Help to Buy, it's possible to get what is effectively a 95% LTV mortgage for your own home. However, if you want to take out a buy to let mortgage, the LTV is typically around 75%. It is possible to get more from a few lenders, but the interest rate won't be very competitive.

Right, that's the bad bit out of the way. Now the really good thing about a buy to let mortgage is that you can get one on an interest-only basis. This is important because paying off capital on a property you plan to exit from in the long term is not necessarily the wisest thing to do.

The more money you sink into the property through finance payments the less money you will have to build your portfolio. If we assume that the value of property always increases over the long term, then paying off the loan is not as important as paying off the mortgage on your own home when it's time to retire. In fact, if you build a property portfolio in the right way, you should make enough to pay off your mortgage and all your obligations and look forward to a comfortable retirement!

TIP: *Try to put in as little of your own money as possible, so that you maximise the benefit from leveraging the bank's money.*

As your property grows in value over time, assuming the figures still stack up for your investment, you may be able to re-mortgage and release all your capital, so you're left with something that makes you money, funded entirely by the bank!

Types of buy to let mortgage

As with a standard mortgage, you will be met with a choice of different types of buy to let mortgage when you go to meet with your bank, broker or IFA. You can get either a fixed rate, variable rate or tracker mortgage. Be careful which one you choose and make sure that it fits with your investment plan.

For example, a mortgage that tracks the base rate when there is a potential increase on the horizon may not be the most sensible decision. You could end up paying more than you budgeted for if the economy starts to do well. On the other hand, you will be quids in if you fix your mortgage while interest rates are low and then the base rate rises..

The product that's right for you will depend on your plans and financial goals, which is why it's important to talk it through with a qualified, independent professional, who can look at all the rates available in the marketplace and help you make the best choice.

Switching your standard mortgage to a buy to let

In recent years we have seen the rise of the 'accidental landlord', where people who are unable to sell their home due to market conditions decide to rent it out so they can move on. To do this, the standard mortgage on the property must be switched to a buy to let mortgage or there must be a 'consent to let' agreement with the lender.

If you can find tenants who will cover the mortgage payments and generate a monthly income for you on top, then this may turn out to be a happy accident and a route into becoming a serious buy to let investor.

However, there may be a few hoops you need to jump through prior to switching to a buy to let mortgage.

Your lender will want to know how much equity, if any, you have in your property and they will also want to know that the likely rental income will more than cover your mortgage payments before they allow you to switch.

You will need to do this even if you just want to 'tread water' with a consent to let, until the market for selling picks up. Your bank may charge one month's mortgage per annum or a higher interest rate for allowing you to go down this route, so it's advisable to raise the deposit you need and switch to a buy to let mortgage as soon as possible.

Why a mortgage broker plays such an important role in your success

If you want to make a success of investing you need to engage someone to advise you on the financing of your investments, but what does mortgage broker actually do for you?

The two most important things a mortgage broker will do for you is save you time and money. Spending too much of your own time and money are two of the biggest threats to your success as a property investor.

Just as you might hire an electrician to do the wiring on your house or a mechanic to fix your car, a broker should be an expert in finding the best possible buy to let mortgage deal.

They will also be able to find that mortgage for you quite quickly and it will be based on the best product for your circumstances. They should also have great relationships with lenders and be able to move you through the process quickly, from application to offer.

I know a few people who tried to go it alone and used the internet to find what they thought were the cheapest products. They mistakenly thought that all a broker does is work off a list of lenders and offer the product that pays the best commission. Maybe that was the case in the old days, but now it's a much more transparent process.

You can actually find yourself much worse off in the long run by going for what appears to be the cheapest deal, only to find that buried in the small print are hefty fees and penalties you may not have picked up on.

A good broker will always show you how much money they'll make for recommending a particular mortgage to you. Even so, it's still worth doing your own research and taking recommendations from other investors. While every broker will advertise themselves as 'always on the end of the phone', you can guarantee most won't be.

You may come across young brokers in sharp suits who seem to know what they're talking about, however it may be wiser try to look for someone who has more experience. When it comes to experience, there is no substitute, particularly if you're looking to build a portfolio.

Hiring a broker is a particularly wise move for high net worth investors. The number of products available to you will be highly competitive and a broker from one of the top firms will be able to give you access to the best deals that won't necessarily be on the 'open market'.

Of course, brokers will charge a fee for their services but the amount of money they will save you in the long term, not to mention the pain and hassle, will be worth it.

If you need some guidance on finding the best broker here are my seven tips:

1. Research well and do your homework
2. Choose a recommended firm
3. Find a broker who will take your calls – even out of office hours

4. Look for someone with a proven track record
5. Present yourself as knowledgeable
6. Have an investment plan in mind to save time (good brokers are busy brokers)
7. Prepare all the information required in advance

If you follow each of these tips, your broker will take you more seriously and you should get a high quality of service.

To pay a fee or not to pay a fee? That is the question...

When you first start searching for a broker you will come across many who will either charge you a considerable fee up front, a modest fee or no fee at all. And it can be difficult to judge which it's best to go with if you're purely searching on the internet.

The broker firms that come top on a Google search are not necessarily the best ones - they might simply have the best websites and employ an SEO company to achieve good rankings.

You need to ask the broker if they are 'whole of market' or not. If they are tied to certain lenders and not truly independent, then they will probably be cheaper than a whole of market broker, but they will make up their commission somehow.

Sometimes paying a fee up front will get you access to deals that could save you more than 20% a month on your repayments – a saving that will cover the fee many times over.

TIP: *Make appointments with several different brokers.*

If you don't currently know any mortgage brokers yourself, nor anyone that can recommend one, then make sure you speak to several and don't just go with the first one who seems to know what they're talking about.

It shouldn't cost anything for guidance on the amount you can borrow, so have a few conversations and get a feel not only for how good they are, but also for their personality. Rapport is important in this business and you want to work with people you like and trust.

Chapter 4

Finding A Property

The million-dollar question in this business is: where do you find a good investment property?

On your property investment journey, you will come across a lot of people who will advise you where they think you should be buying. Being a full-time investor means that I get approached every day by all sorts of people, telling me where the next big opportunity is.

Some of these will be genuine opportunities, but often, if the opportunity seems too good to be true, it probably is. Sometimes it means that the person giving you advice stands to gain more from your investment than you do.

This is why I always recommend doing your own research and building a good relationship with an estate agent. There are plenty of online property companies around who charge what is called a 'finder's fee' for helping you find a property and they will inevitably also take a commission on the sale.

Dealing directly with a reputable estate agent is a much more transparent process and I would strongly advise forming a long-term relationship with one or two agents in the areas where you want to invest. You should be the one seeing the full benefit of any profits to be gained from your buy to let investment and not be forced to share them with a third party.

This book should be a useful tool in your research, helping guide you on what to look for in a good investment property. (What it **isn't** is a one-stop shop filled with everything you need, so you're going to have to take some more time to do all your homework!)

When you're starting out, the right property can be just down the road from where you live. Local knowledge is absolutely vital if you want to find the right investment, so talk to lettings and sales agents to find out what's available and what's in demand and get to know your own specific market. There is also a good deal of information on the internet, including land registry data telling you how much properties have been bought and sold for in the past.

Over several years as a property investor, one of the things I've learned is that property, like any other investment, is not really about what someone tells you; it's more about learning for yourself, trusting your judgement and having the right people to turn to for advice when you need it.

'Success' in property is about finding the investments that fit your plans for the future. I can't tell you what those are and neither can anyone else. Everyone's goals will be different and what makes the right kind of property investment for one person may not be right for you.

It follows, then, that the best place to invest in property for you may be somewhere very different to where I would choose. So if you have someone telling you where to invest, you run the risk of ending up disappointed and with a property that doesn't do for you what you need it to.

What every investor does have in common is a vision of what the perfect investment looks like for them. You just need to be prepared for the possibility that, once you've done the cold hard numbers, the reality might be somewhat different to your dream! The answers to two key questions are critical to your success:

- What level of rents are tenants prepared to pay to live in your property?
- Is the rental return sufficient to cover the mortgage?

The best place to invest for some people is a beaten up old property in a promising area of town. The best place for others will be a property requiring very little work or personal input. The latter generally comes at a premium unless you're very lucky. Remember, you are not the only investor out there and a lot of people are involved in the buy to let business.

Successful investors usually go with what is familiar to them. It's far better to invest in something you know than to venture into the unknown. And property is no different.

New or old property – which is best?

Ultimately, which is best will come down to whichever fits the figures, but everyone has an inclination towards one or the other that shouldn't necessarily be disregarded.

If you're more inclined towards an older property, then you're likely to have to do some work to do to get it ready for letting. You will also be more likely to be a property developer as well as an investor - someone who likes to manage the process, from the building and refurbishment work to the point where you let the property and move on to the next one.

This type of property investment may be particularly suited to you if you're a hands-on kind of person. You might even work in the building trade or have some particular skills related to it so that you're able to keep costs down. But be warned: it used to be the case that you could do up a property to a just-about-habitable standard and tenants would happily move in, but this is certainly not the case any more.

Yes, hiring tradespeople to renovate or refurbish your property can be expensive if you don't fancy joining in yourself, but it's important that you do a good job. Lettings regulations and local council requirements are tightening all the time, so you must make sure the property you're letting is up to scratch.

I've seen tenants happily living in houses with kitchen units falling apart, boilers on the point of breakdown, and water coming in through the windows. However, this kind of tenant is certainly the exception, rather than the rule, and if you don't provide a decent standard of accommodation, you can't expect to get a decent level of rent in return.

If you happen to be investing in sought-after areas, people will have higher expectations than your average tenant and even the slightest thing can put them off.

Older properties in particular can begin to look pretty shabby if they have not been looked after. On the other hand a sensitively-restored property, or the kind of houses you might see on *Grand Designs,* not only look good, the investment in getting it right from the beginning will pay off in the property gaining more value over time.

Of course, all this depends on the kind of budget you have for the work and how long it will take to cover those costs and make a profit - something that should always be your primary focus as a buy to let investor.

If you don't fancy the hassle of renovation or refurbishment, there is always the option of buying new – either already constructed or off-plan.

The advantage of buying new property is that you won't use up any of your spare time doing work and it can be marketed after exchange for tenanting immediately on completion, so you start bringing in rental income right away. The disadvantage is you will inevitably be paying a premium for that pleasure. If the property market is picking up, developers will be inflating their prices to make as much profit as they can.

You will also almost inevitably have other hidden costs to deal with. Unlike the old days, where builders would build the property and move on, most are now part of larger companies that want to continue generating income from their build.

This income is often generated by the builder retaining the freehold and charging you ground rent. You can apply for the freehold, of course, but you may not get it. This is particularly so in the murky world of new apartment blocks, something I'll cover in more detail in Chapter 6.

TIP: *If you want to buy new build, offer either early, when the project is still at the planning stage, or at the end, when there are only a couple of units left.*

Developers will be keen to pick up some sales momentum at the planning stage and then will be motivated to close the project off at the end so they can move on to the next one. In both cases, you may be able to negotiate on price.

If you do decide to invest in a new development, ask yourself the following questions before you sign on the dotted line:

- Does this look like a quality development?
- Can I realistically expect tenants will want to live here, i.e. is it close to town and transport links?
- Does this developer have a strong track record?
- What are the management costs likely to be? Are they realistic?

What makes a bad investment property?

So you have the money to invest in your first buy to let property, but you're not quite sure what makes a good one.

Hunting for an ideal investment property can be time consuming and the best advice I can give is to use a good estate agent who understands exactly what you're looking for and can introduce you to great potential investments as soon as they come to market – or even before. They will also be able to help you avoid some of the classic mistakes that people make when they buy investment property.

Avoiding bad locations

As a buy to let investor, you should make sure you don't have any kind of emotional attachment to the property you're looking to make money out of. This is not your home, it's purely an investment vehicle.

A bad location, from an investment perspective, doesn't necessarily mean the area is run down or undesirable, it simply means it's not going to make you money. So if you buy a property simply because you think it looks really nice, or it reminds you of a house you once lived in yourself, or it seems like a quality area, you're in danger of falling into the bad location trap.

Bad buy to let locations are areas where tenant demand is weak or non-existent. That may be because they're several miles away from the nearest town or city or a decent school, or because the transport links are not good.

You need to focus on the potential of a location to generate a decent rental income and also capital growth on your investment. Properties in locations that don't look so good can be goldmines if enough people want to live in them. The two key things you need to focus on are:

- What is the history of house prices and rental values in the area?
- Is there a good rental demand that is likely to continue?

You can get the answers to both those questions online and by speaking to good local sales and lettings agents.

Example: expensive property, average location, bad investment

Depending on your budget, it's unlikely that you'll find a perfect property that ticks all the boxes. As with anything in life, there will be elements of risk and compromise. You will need to calculate all potential risks very carefully before investing and make sure you research an area thoroughly, because getting the location wrong can be a disaster.

Mr Edwards decides to purchase a penthouse apartment for £250,000. It's in the town centre and very close to local amenities, including a shopping centre, three supermarkets and some coffee shops. On top of this, several other new homes are being built in the town as the developers move in.

The apartment is kitted out to a high standard and the development itself is the literally the talk of the town. Surely Mr Edwards has landed himself the ideal investment property?

Sadly, Mr Edwards has missed some vital clues as to how viable this investment property is from a buy to let perspective.

The first is that, unfortunately, property prices in other towns and cities nearby have always risen higher than here. Even though this town appears to be 'up and coming', it has a reputation for being unfashionable and has always lagged behind a more popular urban area just a short drive away.

The second thing is, unfashionable areas are unfashionable for a reason. They tend to be low income areas, often associated with problems such as higher than average crime rates, overcrowded schools and high unemployment.

Mr Edwards' investment is a bad one because his potential tenant pool will be extremely small to non-existent. People who want decent penthouse apartments don't tend to want them in unfashionable areas and certainly won't be prepared to pay a good price for a bad location, no matter how nice the décor. The property is simply too expensive for its setting, so capital growth will be sluggish at best - at worst, it will go into reverse.

A bad investment property won't make you money even if it could make you a good home. If you really care about making a return, ditch the emotion and take a very close look at all aspects of the area you're about to invest in, particularly average rental returns, demand for sales and lettings, likely capital growth and crime levels.

Buy to Let Checklist

Use the following checklist as a guide to help you choose your next property. This is a simplified version of a spreadsheet I have used myself, so I'd suggest you use it as a starting point to create your own detailed spreadsheet where you can log specific data.

	Good	Average	Poor
Location			
Price (relative to local market)			
Likely rental return			
Capital growth prospects			
Crime rate data			
Historic house price growth			
Local schools			
Perception of the area			
Employment levels			
Universities			
Hospitals			

There is a huge amount of property price and local information available online - I find these websites particularly useful:

Zoopla.co.uk
Rightmove.co.uk
Mouseprice.co.uk
Crimemaps.org.uk

Use these online resources, together with your own local research 'on the ground' to arm yourself with as much knowledge as possible.

If anything, it is much easier to avoid a bad investment property than it has been in the past, simply because there is so much data available now online. The resources are there, all you need to do is use them and you will be well on the road to investment success.

Chapter 5

How And Where To Find A Bargain

You can always find a bargain property but there are certain times during the property market cycle when you are more likely to find one. The best times are during a prolonged slump and when a market is just beginning to take off. The window of opportunity when you can bag yourself the best bargains will be small, so it helps to look for those little signals that present themselves, often in the media and also just by looking around you.

Some people are only happy when they have some bad news to talk about and you will hear a lot more from them during a property market slump. What doom mongers have to say about the market is more likely to have a psychological effect on people's buying and selling habits than when everything looks rosy.

Likewise, when the property market is picking up, you will hear less from the doom mongers and a lot more from the people who are interested in selling property. The press often relies on those with a vested interest in selling property for their news stories (i.e. estate agents and developers), so you often get exaggerated tales about house prices soaring. The thing is, people still believe the papers and what they read online.

In a down cycle...

In a down cycle fear tends to grip a nation. It leaves people thinking, "Will I ever be able to sell my house?", "How much will prices fall?" and the most dangerous thought of all, "If I don't sell now and quickly, I'll be stuck". It's this kind of urgent desperation that leads people into making rushed decisions. This is the time when you can come in with a 'cheeky' offer that would give you great instant equity - and you're more likely to agree a sale in your favour, as you're in a position to meet their needs.

The start of a housing boom

If the market is beginning to 'boom' as investors call it, sellers will be panicking for an altogether different reason. They don't want to miss out on their onward purchase, so again there is urgency to agree a sale quickly before that new home they want is priced out of reach or somebody else gets there first.

So how do you find these 'motivated sellers' and land yourself a property discount?

The answer is, your estate agent. They have access to far more properties than you could hope to find yourself and will have a relationship with their vendors. That puts them in a great position to recommend you as a solid buyer. They will also be able to offer you a wealth of knowledge about a property and its location. Good agents love good investors and are almost always very happy to give free advice on the best areas to buy or at least provide a solid starting point for you to do your own research.

In my experience, it's best to be direct and honest with estate agents about what you're looking for and, on the whole, even if the agent has a vested interest in selling the property, they will give you some hints and clues as to whether this is the right one for you. If they think you're serious about investing and you ask the right questions then you should get some honest answers in return.

Negotiating: right property right price

To be as successful as you can be, you need to work on becoming a skilled negotiator who can drive down the asking price. Unless you happen to be investing in an area where demand is particularly high or people feel 100% confident that they can achieve their asking price, you should be able to get a discount.

Negotiating a discount is an easy way to make money at a very early stage in the process of securing your investment. You can lock in several thousand pounds' worth of equity, simply by negotiating a price reduction of 5-10%.

Unfortunately, not every vendor is prepared to drop their price. There will be some who are not in any particular hurry to sell, in which case, you'll need to have really done your research on the area, into how much similar properties have actually sold for in past 12 months or so. If there are a whole bunch of properties of a similar spec selling for a particular price, then you know that this is likely to be the vendor's bottom line, even if the asking price is inflated.

Remember, the vendor is just as keen as you to walk out of the negotiation with a few thousand pounds more than they started with. That being said, the asking price is the starting point for your negotiation and shouldn't (in most cases) be what you necessarily end up paying.

The main weapons in your armoury going into the negotiation will be time, information and cash. A buy to let investor should have more time on their hands than a typical homebuyer who probably has only a few months to move house.

The process of negotiation should start with having good knowledge of the local market, right down to what is referred to as the 'micro market'. Keep the comparables you use as close as possible in style, size and location to the property you intend to buy. This is the information you need to support your offer, i.e. justify why you're offering that amount.

If the vendor refuses to negotiate then it's best to move on. There will be plenty more opportunities to find a seller who is prepared to drop their price. There's no sense in losing money by paying more than the property is worth and, armed with your research on local prices, you should come across as a serious buyer.

Sometimes you may find that there are no real comparables and the most recent data on house sales is more than 12 months old. In this case, you need to be thinking about making that offer of 5-10% less than the asking price. The vendor may be testing the market and you might just get the discount.

When it comes to negotiating a deal, remember that time is more likely to be on your side and, therefore, the power.

Buying at auction

I would never recommend buying at auction to anyone starting out as a property investor, even though it might seem like a great way to find a bargain.

If what you're buying is cheap, then there has to be a reason why. Generally, if it's been put up for auction, a property will have been on the market for some time and/or the owners are in a hurry to sell.

The main question to ask is why is this property up for auction? Why could it not have been sold through an estate agent?

There are several possibilities:
1. The owner can't sell it
2. The owner needs a quick sale
3. The property needs a lot of modernisation
4. There is a problem with the property
5. The refurbishment costs outweigh the benefit of owning it
6. The property has been repossessed
7. The owner is deceased

If you do decide to take the risk and buy at an auction you will, in almost every case, be buying a property that needs refurbishment work, so you should always get a survey done beforehand to make sure there are no nasty surprises. (If you require a mortgage for the purchase, your lender will have insisted on at least a valuation report and possibly a more detailed survey.)

The problem is, even if you do get the survey done prior to auction, you can't guarantee that you'll have the winning bid. And this isn't the only thing that can't be guaranteed.

Take the story of one unfortunate investor, who decided to bid at auction for a Victorian property in an upmarket area with spectacular views of the sea. It sounded like the perfect investment and it was available for just £38,000.

The auction catalogue at the time mentioned that the property needed extensive modernisation. The investor no doubt thought that at such a low price it wasn't worth getting a survey done and decided to take the risk instead.

A week after he made the winning bid for the property it had disappeared. The local council had decided that the structure of the building was unsound and arranged for its demolition.

The unfortunate investor was left to pay the £38,000 PLUS the demolition bill!

This begs the question, did the seller know that they would be liable for these costs and opt to mislead the buyer? *Caveat emptor – buyer beware. Auctions are the ideal place to get rid of problem properties because the onus is on the buyer to check all the particulars before they part with their cash.*

TIP: *Once you're in the auction room, set the maximum you're prepared to pay and stick to it*!

It's easy to get carried away competing against another bidder. Paying over the odds for a property means it will take longer for you to realise a profit on your investment, if there is any to be had.

Buying at auction with a mortgage

If buying at auction is risky when you have the cash, then buying at auction without any is even more of a gamble!

The minimum amount you need in cash to even consider buying at an auction is 10% of the value of the property you are hoping to buy. So if it's £100,000, then you will need to have your £10,000 ready because you will be contractually bound to pay this when the hammer falls.

If you haven't arranged a mortgage prior to the auction, you will then have a very anxious 28 days waiting for your offer – a wait that could be in vain, as most lenders will take longer than that to approve a mortgage. This leaves you at risk of losing your deposit and if anything should happen to the property in the meantime, you will be liable for any damage as well.

Ultimately, if you're serious about making a success of buy to let you would be wise to avoid anything that creates unnecessary risk and that includes auctions. Remember, there will always be plenty of properties out there that will generate the kind of returns you want.

Buying from a property investment agent or consultancy

The birth of buy to let in the mid-1990s spawned the birth of a whole industry built around property investors. Unlike the traditional estate agent, property investment agents and consultants only deal with investors and offer select opportunities in the UK and overseas.

The investment consultancy will help developers market property investment opportunities to a wider audience. Often, a network of several agents will be marketing the same projects via websites, email and other online marketing channels.

The quality of agents varies. Virtually anyone can set up a website offering property investments and not all the people who run them are trustworthy. You should always research the company and find out whether they are members of organisations such as the AIPP. That's one step to finding out if a company is legitimate, although it's still no guarantee that you won't encounter problems. There are many, many stories of investors losing money through projects being delayed or scrapped, or simply through not getting anywhere near the returns they were told they would.

Property agents make their money through commissions paid by developers on each sale and usually help with client mortgages and paperwork. Although they're ever so friendly while the deal is being agreed, agents usually pay far less attention to investors after their money has been handed over.

Investment agents deal in all areas of residential and, increasingly, commercial property, such as fractional ownership of hotel rooms or student properties. There is usually the promise of high yields and/or high capital growth, plus 'guaranteed' rental returns.

TIP: *Always be wary of any rental guarantees on offer*

They're usually just funded by the inflated purchase price you paid in the first place and when the guaranteed rental period ends, you can soon find that your returns plummet.

As a new investor starting out, the offers can sound tempting and some do turn out to be good investment opportunities. However, it's vital that any investment you make has been thoroughly researched beforehand and you've done your due diligence. These companies will usually tell you there's a limited offer or put some other kind of time pressure on you, to make you think you need to act quickly. If an offer sounds too good to be true, then it is, even if a glossy brochure or website suggests otherwise, and don't ever let yourself be persuaded to short-cut your research for fear of missing the deal of a lifetime. There will always be another deal.

My personal advice is to give these companies a wide berth. With a little research, you can avoid wasting your cash on a go-between and source properties yourself or use an estate agent who only gains from the actual sale of a property rather than a complex commission structure.

Chapter 6

Types of Investment Property

Apartments

Buying an apartment can either be a good investment or the worst you will ever make, depending on where it's located and, just as importantly, how the apartment building is managed.

What's good about apartments?

Apartments are usually low maintenance compared to investing in a house. The cost of external repairs is often shared amongst the community, as are boiler repairs if the block runs off a shared boiler.

Depending on the type of development, apartments might not have a garden or other external space to manage or maintain as would be the case with most houses, so there will be less to factor into your investment forecast when it comes to overall maintenance.

If you invest in an apartment that's close to town and in a relatively good area with easy access to shops, then you're likely to find a tenant pretty quickly. Rental demand is generally good for 2-bedroom apartments that are popular with young professionals, particularly if the apartment has allocated parking, rather than communal or on-street parking.

The value of apartments also tends to lag behind houses in the same area, so the mortgage will cost less a month than it would for a house for a comparable rental return.

What's bad about apartments?

Investing in apartments is rarely as simple as it sounds and if you're thinking of investing in an apartment that is part of a larger dwelling, there are inevitably hidden costs.

Monthly service charges are a virtual certainty if the apartment is leasehold and, unlike buying a house with clear title that you own, you will never be fully in control of your investment. If the company that owns the development chooses to, they can set service charges higher. If the building is run and managed by a residents' committee, any decisions will be made on a majority vote and some of these decisions – which you might not personally agree with - can end up costing large sums of money.

If you decide to invest in a leasehold apartment, you will also be charged a ground rent which tends to be paid annually or every six months. You may also be required to pay money into a sinking fund which helps pay for repairs and upkeep of the building.

If you are still able to make a profit when all these costs are taken into consideration, then an apartment can make a good investment, particularly if it's in a sought-after area of a town or city.

Hotel rooms

Hotel rooms, or fractional ownership of hotel rooms, is a type of commercial property investment that tends to have a lower entry point than a residential investment.

This works on the basis that the investor buys a hotel room or a share of the hotel room (fractional ownership) and gets a share of the profit from guests who stay in the room in return.

The term of this type of investment is typically 10 years and they often come with some form of buy-back guarantee that promises a lump sum if you hand the room back at the end of the 10-year period.

Things to watch out for with hotel room investments

With hotel rooms, you're essentially helping the hotel company build the rooms, so there could be a significant period of time between you committing your funds and the completion of the hotel. That means your money is tied up and you're not getting any returns.

Secondly, unlike buying a conventional property, you will not be able to buy hotel rooms with a mortgage, so it's all your own cash at stake. And working out how the investment stacks up can be tricky, as the calculations of returns can be complex and there is uncertainty if occupancy rates are lower than expected. The risk here is that, unlike a straightforward residential property investment, you're relying on someone else to make a success of the business and manage it properly.

When it comes to exit time, even if the hotel company buys back the room, they're only going to buy it back for what it *was* worth a decade ago, rather than what it's likely to be worth when you want to sell it. With this investment, there is no chance of benefiting from any capital growth.

If you do decide that hotel room investments are a hassle-free way to generate a bit of income and you're willing to take the risk in the long term, then it's important to check the terms of agreement very carefully. Sometimes the returns you get are hardly worth the investment you put in and you may be better off putting your cash elsewhere.

Houses in Multiple Occupation (HMOs)

You can read about HMOs in a lot more detail in my first book, **'HMO PROPERTY SUCCESS'**. For the purposes of this book, I'll briefly summarise what HMOs are and why they can generate more income than other types of buy to let property.

With an HMO you're essentially letting a house room by room to separate individuals, rather than having one tenant or their family occupying the whole house. The properties usually offer five or six private bedrooms and then communal cooking, living and washing facilities.

This set-up can be achieved by buying a three or four bedroom house and then converting a lounge, dining room - or even garage - into bedrooms. There is no law that says a house must have a lounge *and* a dining room, so, if the house is large enough, you should be able to divide it up more or less as you wish, subject to any building, planning and health and safety regulations.

With HMOs you can make two or three times the income you would generate from letting the same property as a single unit. The rental income you make will cover all your regular outgoings and still leave you a healthy profit on top. The other big benefit is that you rarely get badly affected by voids, as it's highly unlikely half your tenants will choose to leave at the same time. As a general rule of thumb, rooms one to four tend to cover your costs, then rooms five and above are your profit.

Things to watch out for with HMOs

The location is a big consideration for HMOs. Not only do you need to make sure there is the right kind of rental demand, but also you will need to consider the regulations of your local council, as they differ from area to area.

This is the second major thing to be aware of – that HMOs are subject to different licensing, planning and health and safety regulations to single-let properties. If you're interested in this kind of investment, it's a good idea to go to your local council and find out exactly what their policies are, before you invest. Sometimes there are restrictions and demands that can severely impact the viability of your buy to let and you need to be clear on the rules before you commit yourself.

The other thing is to vet your tenants carefully as three to five times the number of people living in a house will usually result in more wear and tear over time, so maintenance costs will be higher. In addition, you should try to make sure, as far as you can, that there won't be any major personality clashes in the house.

The demand for HMOs typically comes from:

> Company lets
> Young professionals who work in cities
> Transient workers who need a temporary place to live
> Students
> Social housing
> Unemployed DSS

With this in mind, you need to decide which type of tenant you would prefer to be dealing with. For example, many investors prefer not to let property to people on benefits or students for fear that they may cause problems. Young professionals and other working adults are usually able to pay higher rent, but the council could give you a more guaranteed regular income stream for taking people on housing benefit. You need to research the demand in your specific area and decide the best options for you.

Student lets

In 2012, a report from the international property agency Knight Frank revealed that there is a structural undersupply of purpose-built accommodation for students in the UK. This has prompted a huge increase in demand for this type of property.

The student property sector managed to outperform all other commercial property classes during the economic downturn. Student applicants have increased dramatically in the last decade, both domestically and from abroad. The number of full-time students in higher education is reported to have risen by 540,000 between 1999 and 2012. This has massively increased demand for accommodation, fuelling a building boom in student housing in university towns and cities across the UK.

The 'traditional student house' with five or six students sharing an old Victorian house is slowly being replaced with a new breed of purpose-built pods designed around what students need from their temporary homes.

As a result, the opportunities in this sector fall into either the traditional 'HMO' type house or the purpose-built block where you can invest in one or a number of student 'pods'. These are typically priced at around £70,000 in cities such as Leeds or Manchester - a lot less than you'd pay for a house or an apartment in the city centre. But, inevitably, there are some drawbacks.

The problem with investing in purpose-built student accommodation

Investments in purpose built student property are set up so that investors can buy one or several student rooms in a block and gain a share of the profit from the rent. The investor buys at a low price and the developer makes their profit from the sale of each of the rooms, so it looks like a win/win.

The thing to watch out for with this type of investment is the likely resale market when you decide to exit. It's unclear what the units will be worth in 10 or 20 years' time, unlike a standard house where you own an asset that will undoubtedly have grown considerably in value over the same period.

In addition, ownership of purpose-built student housing is not as straightforward as it sounds and if you're serious about making money from property, there are probably better opportunities to explore in other sectors.

On the plus side, investing in this kind of student housing will be low maintenance, compared to running a student house, because they will be managed for you. If you're not a hands-on type of investor, this may be an attractive proposition, as you're highly unlikely to ever be bothered with having to sort out everyday repairs.

Care homes

Care homes are a similar type of investment to hotel rooms, where you can invest in a room and take a share of the revenue generated by that room. Only they're not half as exciting or profitable as investing in traditional buy to let property!

Several companies are now marketing care homes as an alternative to traditional buy to let investing, spurred on by predictions that the number of older people in society is rising rapidly as people are living longer.

According to the Office for National Statistics, the number of people aged 65 and over is expected to rise by nearly two-thirds by 2031. This means that there should, in theory, be a greater demand for care homes.

Terra Firma, the company that bought the record label EMI for £3.2 billion in 2007, recently turned their attention to Four Seasons, the UK's biggest care home group. This action boosted the idea that care homes are an emerging investment class.

Beware of the hype around care home investments

There are 24,000 care homes in the UK currently and not all of them are full. In fact care homes are actually closing down in some areas of the UK, which raises the possibility that demand is not yet high enough in some locations to make this type of property a good investment.

If you're convinced by the argument that care rooms will be in high demand in the long term, make sure that you're investing in a high-quality development and that the construction company has a strong track record.

Your investment, in many cases, will be used to fund the construction of a care home, so you'll need to carry out due diligence and check that there is good demand, i.e. enough older people already living in the area or who want to spend their twilight years living there. Most older people prefer a care home out in the countryside.

Again, as with hotel rooms, if you're looking for capital growth, you'll always be far better off investing in a house that you actually own, rather than sharing ownership with other investors and companies who will also be taking a share of the profits.

Renovation projects and older property

Buying an old house, refurbishing it and then letting it out is the most popular buy to let strategy because it works. You just need to be prepared to get stuck in and do some of the work yourself.

The good thing is, if you find a property that needs work, you're unlikely to have a huge amount of competition from other buyers and it will always be cheaper than buying new or nearly new.

The three most important things to consider with a renovation property are:

> The cost of the refurbishment
> The area the property is in
> The type of tenant you're hoping to attract

The days when you could just buy a property, make it habitable and put it on the market are now a thing of the past. This isn't the early '90s any more and even students expect a certain level of comfort.

As jobs have become more mobile these days, there is a chance that your tenant may be looking for a home from home, and they or their companies will be prepared to pay extra to guarantee comfort.

Imagine the following:

Mr Edwards invests £200,000 in a property but it only generates **£800 a month** in rental income because it's in poor condition.

If only he had invested an extra £20,000 in making the property look good, he could have been making £1200 a month.

So the false economy at the beginning means that Mr Edwards is only generating a 4.8% return, as opposed to the 6.5% return he could have generated by carrying out the refurbishment.

If you're not prepared to put in the time and effort to prepare your property properly for rent – and renovation and refurbishment does require effort – it's probably wiser to consider investing in something that just requires a bit of decorating and a lick of paint to get it looking right.

Cheap terraced housing

Terraced housing is cheap for a reason: because it's usually the least desirable type of house. The rooms tend to be small, there are people on both sides and very little privacy, there's rarely any parking and the neighbourhoods are often run-down.

However, many property investors decide to go down the terraced housing route because it is far cheaper than most other property types and the gross rental returns can be high in and around some cities.

Areas where cheaper terraced housing tends to be available are often those populated by people on lower incomes or unemployment benefits. The low purchase price means the investor doesn't need much rental income to still turn a profit, and there's a high demand for cheap housing.

Don't be fooled - cheap terraced housing can be high maintenance

While not all terraced houses are bad investments, if you're investing in inner cities, you stand a good chance of the crime rate being higher than normal and having undesirable neighbours that will put off potential tenants.

Some of the potential pitfalls of terraced housing are:

- ○ Failing to achieve capital growth
- ○ You should expect to have to hold the property for a long time to see returns
- ○ The area may become a ghetto and a focus for crime over time

With the above in mind, it's extra important to find out as much as you can about the area where you intend to buy terraced housing and check that the level of rent you intend to charge reflects what's already being paid each month for other houses on the same street. Also, try to buy in areas that have a visible sense of community.

Buying off-plan

When property prices are rising, there is often a surge in the number of people willing to put down a deposit on a property they've only seen illustrated on paper plans or in a glossy brochure.

During the last property boom in the UK, buying off-plan was seen as the ideal way to secure an investment early at a discounted price and lock in some equity. Some investors were even able to turn a profit before completion, by selling on a property that had risen in value as it was being built.

A major benefit of buying off-plan is that you get to choose your plot early and reserve the best units on a development. As many as 90% of properties may be sold off-plan before there is any visible sign of houses in high demand areas of London and the South East.

There are always 'special offers' with new builds and you may be offered some kind of discount for putting down your deposit early on a property. Just be aware that the 'discount' may not be genuine if the property's true value has not yet been established. And herein lies a big risk when you buy off-plan. If you can't guarantee what the value of the property will be when it completes, then it becomes a bit of a gamble investing your cash.

There is also the very real possibility that property prices may fall while you are waiting for the property to be built.

Case study:

Catherine puts down a 10% deposit on an off-plan house in a new development she has seen in a glossy brochure. She plans to pay off the remainder of what she will owe with finance.

She selects the plot she think would most appeal to tenants. She then arranges a buy to let mortgage to cover the balance, sits back and waits for her investment property to complete.

6 months later something bad happens to the economy and house prices start falling. The property Catherine bought with a discount ends up being valued at less than she agreed to pay for it.

Worse still, her buy to let mortgage was only an agreement in principle, which the bank can amend or withdraw at any time.

Catherine is left with a shortfall. The bank refuses to lend the money and the developer wants to receive the asking price set 12 months earlier.

Fortunately, the developer agrees to take back the property, but on the condition that Catherine pays the difference between what the developer can now sell it for and the original sale price that was agreed 12 months earlier.

Unless she can find a lender willing to give her a mortgage for the agreed amount, Catherine will be left £50,000 out of pocket.

This experience is a worst-case scenario, but it's based on a true story of someone investing just prior to the last credit crunch. Agreements in principle from a lender should never be seen as a guarantee that you will get the money. Always keep an eye out for any signs in the housing market that prices may start to fall or that mortgage interest rates are set to rise – if you have a good broker, they should keep you up to date.

Finally, do be realistic and understand that the finished development itself probably won't look like it does in the brochure, so the best advice is to only buy off-plan with a reputable developer or one that you're familiar with.

But if you really want to make a success of investing in property why take a gamble on off-plan at all? I think it's far better to invest in a house you can see and touch when you agree to buy it, rather than lock in a theoretical discount on a property that may or may not look like an artist's impression.

PART TWO:
MAKING MONEY
FROM PROPERTY

Chapter 7

Generating An Income

How to calculate your rental returns

If you want to make it as a property investor, you need to understand some basic maths. There are many secret formulas and ways to calculate a return on investment and there are plenty of clever people out there who can use maths to convince you that you can get a great return on some of the worst property investments!

Don't take any notice when you see adverts promising huge double-digit net returns or guaranteed rental yields. The reality is often something quite different. Successful property investors are able to calculate returns from property themselves quite easily, using a simple net return calculation.

A gross rental return is the total amount of money your tenant pays you for the pleasure of living in your property. But this isn't what you're going to end up with. Your actual net return – or pre-tax profit – is what you're left with after all your expenses have been taken out.

Here's an example:

A pensioner is selling his flat at a heavy discount due to ill health. He's a distressed seller who needs to sell quickly so he can find more suitable accommodation.

He paid £165,000 for the flat when it was new and has now decided to reduce the price to £100,000 in order to force a quick sale.

The apartment looks like a bargain, one of those rare opportunities to buy at a heavy discount, lock in equity and generate positive cash flow as soon as it's put up for rent.

Other similar-sized apartments in the area are renting for £700 a month.

A buy to let mortgage could be secured on this £100,000 property for £400 a month.

The investor can't lose, right?

Wrong!

Monthly Rental Income: £700
Monthly Mortgage: £350
Monthly income from rent = £350

This is what we call the 'gross' return on this property.

To find the net return we need to look at how much this property will cost us to run.

Owning a property in this block of luxury flats means that there is a high service charge, which has just increased to £250 per month.

So if I were to invest in this apartment, the net return is suddenly looking less appealing:

Monthly Rental Income: £700
Monthly Mortgage: £350
Monthly Service Charge: £250

Monthly profit from the property = £100

£100 a month in positive cash flow isn't too bad, but you will need to put pretty much all of that aside to cover one-off repairs, which can add up to a lot on communal properties. There may also be ground rent to pay and building insurance which, again, could add around £50 a month to your on-going costs.

But this still doesn't tell you the whole story, it only gives you a cash flow figure.

Most property investors talk about yield – that's the cash return as a percentage of the current value of the property. In it's most simple form, as a gross yield figure, it only takes into account the rental income:

Property Value: £100,000
Annual Rental Income: £8,400
Gross Yield: £8,400/£100,000 x 100 = 8.4%

But gross yield doesn't take costs into account. To properly compare properties as investments, you need to use the net profit figure:

Property Value: £100,000
Annual Net Income (profit): £100 x 12 = £1,200
Net Yield: £1,200/£100,000 x 100 = 1.2%

Suddenly that yield figures has fallen dramatically and a property that only gives a net yield of 1.2% is definitely not one you should be investing in unless you've got it at a huge discount and are looking to sell on as soon as the market picks up. You really should aim for a minimum net yield of 5%, to protect yourself against interest rate rises.

While yield allows you to compare one property with another, if you want to be able to compare property with other types of investment, you need to know the return on your invested funds. To calculate the return on investment (ROI) that this £100,000 property will give, you need to factor in the amount you invested to fund the purchase.

Deposit + Purchase Costs = £18,000
Annual Net Profit: £100 x 12 = £1,200
Return on Investment: £1,200/£18,000 x 100 = 6.66%

As you hold your investment, you can add capital growth into your annual profit figure and you should see your ROI steadily increasing.

TIP: *Be clear on your projected net returns (income), yield and total return on investment figures BEFORE you buy.*

The bottom line is, to be successful in buy to let investing, always find out the total costs associated with the property you're planning to buy. That will allow you to calculate what the actual returns will be and compare investment opportunities properly.

How long should you hang on to a property?

If we assume that the price of property in the UK doubles every 10 years, as is often quoted, then holding a property sounds like a no-brainer. Unfortunately, it is not quite as straightforward as that.

It would be more realistic to say prices *can* double every 7 to 10 years, but there is no guarantee. So whether you should buy and hold really comes down to timing. Time it wrong and you will need to hold a property a lot longer to achieve some worthwhile profits and for this you need a long-term strategy.

This is why all the property experts out there will tell you that you should look to hold a property for at least five years and not sell at all unless you really need to. Essentially, buy and hold is proven to be the best way to achieve your primary buy to let investment goal, which is to build wealth from property.

This strategy will always work for you if you can maintain positive cash flow. To do that, you need to invest in the right kinds of investment property that will allow you to generate the level of cash flow you need.

The best kept secret in buy to let

If only everyone was familiar with the magic that can happen over time when you buy and hold a property, then everyone would be a buy to let investor! This magic starts with the way you can leverage your money by borrowing from the bank and, as the property grows in value, use it to buy more properties.

Then there is inflation. While it steadily erodes the value of the money you have borrowed via mortgage finance, property values are steadily increasing, as are rents, which tend to keep track with inflation.

That means in real terms that over time:
- The value of the money you owe the bank drops
- Your rental profits increase
- The capital value increases and you benefit from **all** the

additional equity, not just the increase on your proportion of the invested funds

Therefore your ROI gets better and better.

To give an example:

> Property Value: £160,000
> Mortgage Borrowing at 75% LTV: £120,000
> Annual Interest Only Payment (5%): £6,000
> Annual Rental Income (5% of property value): £8,000
> Year 1 Profit (before any other costs): £2,000

If inflation is running at 3% per annum, your borrowing of £120,000 effectively drops in value by £3,600. That's £3,600 you would have 'lost' if it had been your own money. As it is, it's the bank that's 'losing'.

Assuming property prices are increasing at 5% per annum, in year two of holding your investment:

> Property Value: £168,000
> Mortgage Borrowing remains: £120,000
> Annual Interest Only Payment (5%) remains: £6,000
> Annual Rental Income (5% of value): £8,400
> Year 2 Profit (before any other costs): £10,400 (£2,400 rent, plus £8,000 equity)

ROI Year 1:

      Personal Investment: £40,000

      Annual Profit: £2,000

      Annual ROI: 5%

ROI Year 2:

      Personal Investment: £40,000

      Annual Profit: £10,400

      Annual ROI: 13% (26% across the two years, averaged out)

The reason your ROI looks so healthy is because the power of leverage – which is greater for property than for any other asset class – allows you to benefit from growth on borrowed funds. And this is the magic.

Add further properties to your portfolio and your financial future begins to look very rosy indeed.

Short-term or long-term lets?

Investing in a short-term let can be a good option for a number of reasons. Generally, you would be letting short term if you needed to rent out a property in a hurry and it happened to be in an area where there was a demand for this kind of tenancy.

On the other hand, you may have purchased a holiday property that you plan to use yourself for a few weeks each year and have short-term tenants cover the costs for the remainder. It's possible to short let any type of property, from a studio apartment to a six-bedroom house.

A short-term let will be an agreement for someone to rent a property for less than six months (the standard minimum term for a long-term let). This type of tenant may have a work assignment in the area and they won't want the hassle of finding a property and furnishing it, or paying for a hotel, which can work out as a lot more expensive over the course of a few months.

This type of short-term tenancy arrangement is more common in larger cities than it is in towns and smaller cities, where there is unlikely to be sufficient demand. It can also work well in areas of the country that are popular with tourists - in this case they're more likely to be holiday lets.

Some advantages of short-term lets compared to long-term lets

- You can charge 25% or more extra rent.
- The income you make can more than cover your costs while you're waiting to fill the property long term.
- If you're planning to use the property as a holiday home, short-term letting while you're not there is a great way to cover your costs.

- There is a growing demand in busy city centres, particularly in London. Large companies can supply regular short-term tenants and this can be a more stable option and reduce potential voids.
- It will be easier to raise the rent as you inevitably get more uplift with a high turnover of tenants.

Why it's better to let long term

- The reality is that it's always harder to find tenants looking for short-term rentals. You will be targeting a much smaller sector of the market.
- The costs of running a short-term let will be higher. Tenants on work assignments working for large companies will generally expect a higher standard of accommodation than the 'usual' tenant.
- You will inevitably find that void periods are reduced with long-term lets.
- Short-term lets will take up a lot more of your time than a long-term let, simply because they require more management.
- You only need to provide the basics, such as white goods, in a long-term let.
- Planning for the future is always easier when you know what your income will be six to 12 months in advance.

Buying property with a partner – the pros and cons

Investing in property with a partner, friends or family can sound like an ideal money-making venture. And, provided you start things off in the right way, there is certainly no problem with taking this route into buy to let investing.

If you do decide that, for financial reasons, the only possible way to invest in a property is with a partner, then you'll need to consider the long-term implications of this type of arrangement.

Here's an example to help illustrate why it's so important to get things right from the beginning:

Philip decides to enter into a partnership with his friend, Mike. They have known each other for years and trust has never been an issue between them. Neither has the money to invest in a property that will generate a good rental income, so they decide to look into pooling their money so they can buy together.

The arrangement goes well at first. They agree to split everything 50/50 – both management of the property and the income made from it. This ensures that everything is simple and fair from the outset.

It works okay for the first year. They begin to generate an income from the rent, which covers the costs and leaves them with a modest return on their investment at the end of each month.

Soon after, disagreements start to arise over who is actually in charge. What started out as a partnership soon turns into one partner taking over.

Mike reacts furiously to Philip's attempts to control everything and the arrangement soon begins to unravel. It turns out that one partner is actually more ambitious than the other when it comes to making the most out of the investment and expanding into other properties.

Each partner had their own approach and their differences were irreconcilable. What was a good friendship didn't work well when it came to business.

Sometimes differences won't surface until it is too late and one partner can be left dissatisfied or, worse still, feeling that they have been misled and out of pocket.

Ways to make sure a property partnership works
- Make sure that you have everything down in writing from the beginning.
- Think very carefully before entering into what amounts to a business relationship with friends or family members. The dynamics of a business relationship, will be very different and at times there will be disagreements.
- Invest in one property at a time. That way you can always

keep your exposure to a minimum and invest independently.

○ Whoever you're investing with, make sure that they have some sense of what buy to let investing is all about. Ideally, partner with someone who has some experience.

Chapter 8

Letting Your Property

How to find tenants

The easiest way to find a tenant is by using a letting agent. They will be able to advertise on popular property websites such as Rightmove and Zoopla, which is where most people will be looking for rental properties in the UK.

Letting agent

An established letting agent will also have a shop window where passers-by may see your property advertised. The letting agent will charge you a fee for finding a tenant, however this may well be worth it when you consider the work you would need to do to find one yourself.

Online estate agents

A variety of online estate agents services have sprung up in recent years, which cost less than the high street agency route. This can be a good idea if you want to keep fees to a minimum and get the benefit of free advertising. Beware though, the free advertising will not be on Rightmove or where most of your prospective tenants will be looking, unless you pay for extras, so it may be a false economy.

Social media

Another growing opportunity is via social media channels, including Twitter and Facebook. If you decide to go it alone and look for a tenant yourself, it's entirely possible that with just a few posts on Facebook you'll be handling several enquiries for your property. If you intend to go down this route, bear in mind you'll need a lot of friends who actually read your social updates!

Newspaper advert

A classified advert in the local newspaper is one of the more traditional routes to reaching a large audience and a little out of date. You'll find that newspaper advertising works better in some areas than others, so do a bit of research before you shell out for an advert.

TIP: *Don't forget to carry out tenant checks*

You need to carry out the appropriate checks on your tenant before accepting them into your property. Referencing and credit checks may be conditions of your mortgage or property insurance.

A big advantage of using an agent is that they will take care of this responsibility for you.

Should you engage an agent to find you a tenant or do it yourself?

Unless you really know what you're doing, you should advertise your property with an agent so that the appropriate background checks are made, with references, 3 months' bank statements and previous landlord references stating rents were paid on time.

The main benefit of using an agent to advertise the property for you is that you can keep yourself largely out of the equation when it comes to interaction with your tenants. One of the biggest mistakes landlords make is to become too friendly and fail to clamp down on problems like late payment of rent. Buy to let is a business and there is no room for sentiment when it comes to your cash flow. The agent will be able to organise viewings and show people around – and bear in mind that they're the professionals and know what needs to be said and done.

The prospective tenant will also take an estate agent more seriously when negotiating the rent and following instructions. Estate agents will have a code of practice for dealing with different types of tenants and how to handle them, so it pays to have access to that valuable experience.

Always ensure you use an agent who is a member of ARLA or NALS, as they also have rental insurance to protect your money if anything goes wrong in the business.

How to avoid bad tenants

A bad tenant is something no buy to let investor needs or wants. They either won't look after the property, or won't pay the rent on time - or both. This can have a significant impact on the profitability of your investment and peace of mind.

Don't think for a moment that bad tenants happen to other buy to let investors. 60% of landlords have problems with bad tenants, so the odds are that you'll get one at some point. The important thing is that you make sure all your paperwork is up to date and you know how to deal with problems if they arise.

In some of the worst reported cases, properties have been turned into cannabis farms or brothels, houses have been trashed and landlords have had to deal with lengthy evictions, with rent owed running into the thousands. Even at the tamer end of the spectrum, it was recently reported that 100,000 tenants in the UK had not paid their rent for 2 months. Just a small period of time without rent coming in can make a big impact on your cash flow and if there's damage to repair, you could end up massively out of pocket.

If you've decided to find the tenant yourself, where possible, I would strongly advise setting up a meeting with your prospective tenant, so you can get a feel for the kind of person they are. Find out as much as possible about them and their circumstances before you allow them to move into your property.

Remember, it's easier to keep someone out of your property in the first place than go through costly legal battles to remove them when things go bad, so it pays to use all the means available to help you try to ensure you let to a good tenant.

TIP: *Make sure you have the right insurance cover*

Buy to let investors require specialist landlord insurance, so make sure you have an appropriate policy that covers you for malicious damage by tenants. You may also want to look into rent guarantee insurance options.

Should the property be let furnished or unfurnished?

A lot of the accepted wisdom when it comes to letting out your property these days is that it should be unfurnished. This does, however, depend on the type of tenant you're aiming to attract. Some tenants will almost always require furnished property, primarily:

- Students
- DSS
- Short-term tenants

So, depending on the area and type of properties you're investing in, furnishing a property can either work in your favour or you'll end up spending more money than you should have done. And the latter will eat into your profits!

There are advantages to letting your property furnished. If your prospective tenant sees the property furnished to a high standard, then they may find it more appealing because they'll save money on furniture and the process of moving in will be faster.

Young professionals, in particular, may not want to have to bother furnishing a place themselves if all they want is a temporary base in the city centre close to work.

If, on the other hand, your tenants happen to be a family or couple who want to rent long term, beyond six months, then most investors agree that furnishing the property will make no difference. In fact, it may even put them off if they were hoping to make the property more of their own home.

If you do decide to go down the furnished route, then make sure you do it properly, as tenants are far more discerning than they used to be and landlords are upping their game to make sure they stay competitive. Student properties may not demand the latest in stylish furniture, but it will be easier to attract them if everything is in good repair.

Part furnishing

Part furnishing your buy to let property is a good compromise between spending far too much money and satisfying most tenant types. Putting in white goods and some basics – beds, wardrobes, a sofa, etc. – will mean tenants can move in right away at very little cost, but there's still room for them to bring in their own furniture and furnishings if they want to.

I have heard stories of landlords having to put furniture in storage just because they found a fussy tenant who didn't like their taste. Make sure you're very clear with tenants about what's staying in the property, because storage is expensive and will eat into your profits, unless you can find another home for any unwanted furniture.

What furnishings you should provide in a property

Furniture & appliances	short term tenants/ students	Long term tenants / families
beds	√	X (with some exceptions)
sofa & chair(s)	√	X
table	√	X
wardrobes	√	√
TV	√	X
DVD/CD player	√ (luxury only)	X
cooker	√	√
dishwasher	√ (luxury)	X
fridge freezer	√	√
washing machine	√	√
curtains/ blinds	√	X
microwave	√	X

As a rule of thumb, apartments in city centres will usually require some kind of furnishing while you can probably get away with providing the minimum in larger family houses.

The more equipment you supply your tenant with, the more chance there is that something will get broken. So save yourself a lot of hassle by only providing the minimum amount required. What your tenant doesn't have, they won't miss!

Setting the rent

The easiest way to set the rent on your property is to look at what people are paying for comparable properties in the same area.

There is plenty of information available online these days and it should take less than a few minutes to gauge rental demand by looking at websites such as Rightmove or Zoopla, because nearly every property up for rent in your area will be on these websites. If you're investing in HMOs, you'll find most people look for rooms on SpareRoom.co.uk and EasyRoommate.com.

There isn't much point in guesswork at this stage, because you may end up either setting the rent too high and getting no interest or setting it too low and regretting it later.

If you find yourself struggling to let the property or the phone hasn't been ringing for weeks on end, it could be a sign that you have a lot of competition, even if you think the rent you have set is competitive with other properties in the area. Like any investment, the market can be brutally efficient and will dictate rent levels.

If you own a property that doesn't seem to be attracting tenants, it may be the wrong type of property for a particular area or it may be too far away from local amenities, in which case you'll need to adjust your rent accordingly to avoid lengthy voids. This is why it's so important you take time in the beginning to thoroughly research the area and the demand. Voids are the death-knoll for cash flow and if it turns out you can't charge as much rent as you thought you could, over a sustained period it could seriously impact the viability of your investment plan.

Bear in mind that as long as you're giving tenants what they want, most will happily pay a little more for things like:

- A nice view
- A garden (young families)
- Modern fixtures and fittings
- Good storage
- Extra space
- Higher floors (if apartments)

The goal is to let the property, even if it means taking off that extra profit you were hoping for.

Why setting the right rent is critical to your profit

Before you get to the stage where you're setting the rent, you will hopefully have taken the advice I gave earlier on generating a profit from your investment. Rental income is absolutely critical to this.

The absolutely minimum rental income you should consider when budgeting for your investment is an amount that at least covers your running costs, with money left over to also cover any void periods (the times when you don't have a tenant). It's critical that in your initial planning stages, before you buy, you're satisfied you have an accurate and realistic picture of the rent levels in your area for your specific type of property and that you've calculated the running costs correctly. Getting these figures wrong could be disastrous for your profits.

In the vast majority of cases, renting is not a long-term choice for people and they will leave eventually due to changes in their circumstances. You will be faced with re-setting the rent on your properties every now and then, even if it's just to keep up with inflation.

Of course, the longer you hold a property, the less pressure there is on the rental income, as the effect of inflation slowly works its magic and the capital value rises.

Types of tenancy agreements

Don't get so carried away with your buy to let adventure that you overlook some of the legalities. Lettings regulations are changing and tightening all the time, so making sure you're legally watertight is extremely important. One of the big things to get right is the legal agreement between you and your tenant.

Both you and your tenant have certain rights and responsibilities, whether you have put the tenancy agreement in writing or not, so it makes sense to do the paperwork properly and make sure everyone is clear on the terms.

A tenancy can either be fixed term or short term (week by week, month by month).

The most common tenancy agreement is known as an assured shorthold tenancy agreement or AST. Unless you have been letting out a property since the 1980s or your tenant is paying you over £100,000 a year, the chances are your tenancy agreement will be an AST.

If you use a letting agent, they will take care of all the paperwork as part of the service they provide, including protecting the tenant's deposit and handling all the related administration, but if you've decided to do it yourself, you can find standard ASTs online to download and in larger stationers.

If you are simply using an 'off the shelf' AST, it may be worthwhile speaking to a legal lettings specialist, to make sure all the terms are present and correct for your particular type of property, let and tenant.

Chapter 9

Investing Overseas

Properties by the beach in a warm climate or in some of the world's most attractive cities can be very tempting, but if you're a UK-based investor, how do they stack up as investments against properties closer to home?

A lot of overseas properties look unbelievably cheap compared to what you would pay for the equivalent in the UK. They may come with incentives, such as a rental guarantee, or there might be an appealing extra, such as a pool.

If you're buying a holiday home for yourself, then by all means get carried away, but if you're a serious investor, these considerations are secondary to the question: will I make money out of this property in the long term?

Never invest in a property market you don't understand

Warren Buffett said, "Never invest in a business you can't understand", and that certainly applies to investing in overseas property. Becoming a buy to let investor means that you absolutely have to think like a business owner.

If you don't understand a country or have never even visited it, how can you be sure that you can actually make more of a profit from a property you will rarely get to see, thousands of miles away? You don't know the area, the currency, the economy, even the language may be foreign to you. And then there's the legal system. Buying, owning and operating a buy to let could be very different to doing the same here in the UK.

You will need to arrange a specialist mortgage to invest overseas and if you don't know the country yourself, you'll need to have a trusted professional who does and who can give you good, independent information and advice. This is critical when it comes to all paperwork and financial arrangements.

TIP: *Use your own independent professionals*

If you're buying new or off-plan from a developer or agent, they will have their own team of mortgage brokers, lawyers and surveyors. Whether they're UK based or overseas, always insist on getting a second opinion from an independent professional in each case, to make sure your own interests are being properly taken care of.

On the positive side, investing overseas can certainly pay off in terms of the price you pay for property. In some European countries you could by a small shopping mall for the price of a single property in the UK. Just be very careful to find out why the property seems like such a bargain. Remember, you are going to need to rent it immediately and then sell it at some point in the future, so it's vital you have good evidence that there is – and will continue to be – strong rental and resale markets.

The big wins tend to come from investing early in emerging markets, where the economy and living standards of a population are rising and pushing up prices. In these locations, you might see some spectacular growth in the value of your investment – much higher than can be achieved in the UK.

Just be aware that the investors who really reap the benefits of investing overseas tend to be people who have spent a lot of time and put a lot of effort into analysing the market. They are the ones who know about opportunities at the earliest stages and it's likely that by the time you get to hear about them – certainly by the time there's a glossy brochure – the window for making the best profits has been and gone.

Potential pitfalls of investing overseas

No matter how smooth the salesman or agent has been, don't for a minute expect the process to be plain sailing, if you're dealing with builders, you may need to make frequent trips abroad and if the property is being bought off-plan, delays regularly occur, so you'll need to have a backup plan in case things go wrong.

You could fill a library with stories of people who have lost thousands of pounds or even their life savings through buying property abroad. Whether you're planning to invest in EU countries or beyond its borders, one of the biggest issues you'll face is that of transparency.

The story of the British investors who lost £600,000 in Turkey
One of the most alarming stories I've come across involves a group of investors who lost £600,000 attempting to buy property in a Turkish holiday resort.

The resort was already popular with Brits and this particular group of investors thought they were buying some property as an investment. They were sold the idea that they could invest in the resort for as little as £38,000 per property and benefit from some high returns.

The fraudster, who was actually a UK national, conned her victims by convincing them to invest in a deal that she promised would make them a return in a matter of weeks.

She convinced one investor to lend her £50,000, which she said would generate a 50 per cent profit, i.e. it would come back to them as £75,000 in less than 6 months. The promised returns never arrived. Fortunately, the fraudster was caught and convicted, but it still left the investors significantly out of pocket.

This is an extreme case, however it does highlight the danger of deals that look too good to be true and of presuming that when you're abroad, somehow there's less need for diligence. Far too many investors still think, "Oh, that's just how they do it out here..." and accept what they're told by whoever's flogging the deal, because they don't know what they're doing. And that brings me back to my earlier point: never invest in a market you don't understand. You need to be extra vigilant when investing overseas and if you invest outside the EU there are even more potential pitfalls.

Travelling to and from a property overseas, the costs can certainly add up. It can also be time-consuming, particularly if you need to obtaining residents permits (outside the EU), where you may be required to pay a fee for staying longer than a few weeks.

In terms of your profits, have you investigated and understood currency exchange rates and the tax implications both of making money in another country and of bringing your profits back to the UK? You may think you're doubling your rental profits or capital growth by investing overseas, but those profits can easily be wiped out if the exchange rates go against you and you're required to give a large chunk of money over to HMRC.

Another important thing to consider is the long-term potential and the security of your investment. How much protection do you have in place in the event that things go wrong?

Political and economic stability in your chosen country is of vital importance. As we have seen in recent years, even Europe is not immune to conflicts and civil wars - as the near-economic collapse of Greece and Cyprus recently demonstrated. If you're thinking of extending your adventure beyond Western Europe these are legitimate concerns and you don't want to be having sleepless nights thinking about them.

While the UK economy will fluctuate, it is a reasonably stable and safe market, unlikely to ever experience the volatility you see in some other countries. You'll never get the huge price rises of emerging markets, but then you'll never get the crashing lows either.

PART THREE:

MANAGING YOUR INVESTMENT PROPERTY

Chapter 10

Being A Landlord

It's a great feeling when you invest in your first property. But now comes the hard bit: being a landlord. You've got to decide how the property will be let and managed and how to deal with tenants who may not always be the kind of people you imagined.

Should you manage the property yourself or use an agent?

If you want to grow a buy to let business, you have to learn to delegate. One of the things I learned when starting out in business was that there are always certain tasks that are better given to someone else, either to save you time now or money in the long term. You're in this business to make money, so you need to balance cutting out any unnecessary costs that might negatively impact on your monthly profits, while recognising that paying for a good service is likely to reap rewards over the longer term.

Trying to do everything yourself can actually end up costing you more and hold you back from what you're trying to achieve in property investment. How many successful entrepreneurs do you know who do their own accounts, cleaning and administration?

There is lot more to running a buy to let property than simply arranging a mortgage and getting a tenant in. There's the marketing of the property and tenant referencing, lettings regulations you must comply with, legal processes and paperwork that must be administered correctly, maintenance requirements, a variety of issues and complaints that might need to be handled...the list goes on. And all these various tasks that are best handled by an experienced professional, not to mention the advantage that a lot of the legal liability for paperwork, deposit protection, etc. falls to them, not you.

There are, of course, both pros and cons to hiring an agent and I think that when you're starting out, it's helpful to work with someone who knows what they're doing.

As I've built my portfolio, I've gradually employed a team of people to let and manage my properties for me, so I no longer use a letting agent. However, what works for me may not necessarily work for you, and if you only have one or two properties and/or don't have the time to focus on the administration of your investments, then an agent is probably the right route for you. Either way, I know that I, personally, would not have made it this far or been as successful as I have without help from trained professionals.

Advantages of doing it yourself

You save money on letting agent fees.

There is no question that a letting agent will take a significant chunk of the money you make from letting your property – usually somewhere between 10% and 15% of the monthly rental income for a full letting and management service.

So if your property is renting for £800 a month, you will only see £680 to £720 of that money – and remember that some agents will also charge set-up fees, inventory fees and tenant checking fees when there is a change of tenancy.

You choose the tenants.

If you like to be hands on, then at least you can choose your own tenants. Remember that you will need to do background checks, immigration status checks and ask for reliable references. Appearances can be deceptive, as the old saying goes, so make sure that you are completely happy before you allow someone to live in your property. Do bear in mind that credit checking and referencing may be a condition of your mortgage or insurance.

You will be more involved in what's happening.

It won't be physically possible for your letting agent to regularly check every property on their books, so none of them will be able to do it as often as you can. You may also be able to build a better relationship with your tenant than they might have with an agent and respond faster and more efficiently to any problems the tenant might have.

Disadvantages of doing it yourself

You will end up committing far too much of your valuable time.

You may still have a job or your rental property could be some distance from your home, so managing it yourself could mean spending lots of time travelling around.

Things can go wrong at any time and you will have to drop whatever you're doing to deal with issues. And while the property is being marketed, there's all the to-ing and fro-ing for viewings – for which prospective tenants sometimes don't even show up! – not to mention the time you'll need to spend on administration.

The lettings agent, on the other hand, will have a reliable set of tradespeople to take care of things like the gas, electrics, plumbing, repairs and decorating. If you're a DIY expert yourself, you may feel able to tackle a lot of maintenance yourself, but what happens when you have a large portfolio of properties?

You're liable for complying with all the lettings regulations

One of the biggest benefits of using an agent who is a member of

ARLA or NALS is that they are kept up to date by their regulatory body or association on all changes to lettings regulations. They have insurance and legal advice on tap.

Unless you're absolutely confident that you have the time and know-how to keep on top of legislation and understand how to make sure you and your properties remain compliant, I'd say this is a big argument for not doing it yourself.

You don't have the benefit of training and experience.
Agents let and manage properties all day long. They know the local market inside out, they're up to date with what tenants need and want and they've handled pretty much every problem that could come up. They know how to resolve issues and carry out evictions. If you try to handle everything yourself from the outset, you're going to end up learning some hard and possibly expensive lessons.

Every time you need professional advice you'll have to pay for it, whereas if you use a reputable agent, most will happily give you free advice, about your let, the market and buy to let in general. Don't underestimate the value of experience.

...and a final advantage of using an agent
You can reduce your tax liability! Your letting agent fees can be offset against your rental income, which means HMRC will

effectively help pay for the management of your properties. So the more properties you have, the more money you can put to better use.

Dealing with problem tenants

Problem tenants can be a real nightmare. The more properties you have, the greater the risk of finding one, so it's very important that you have a plan in place to deal with the most common problems.

Dealing with late rent or non-payment

One of the biggest headaches you will encounter is tenants not paying their rent on time – and there are more of them doing this than you might think. 100,000 tenants in the UK had not paid their rent for 2 months, according to a recent study - and they're only the cases that were reported; there are no doubt plenty more on top of that.

Sometimes tenants genuinely simply fall on hard times and unemployment is a major factor, particularly in tough economic times. But much of the time, when tenants are late paying rent or stop paying entirely, it's because they're either bad at managing their money, or they think they can get away with it.

Regardless of the reason, when tenants fall behind with their rent, you need to act quickly. If you use an agent, they will chase the tenant up for you and issue notices and demands as necessary. However, if you're managing the property yourself and have a relationship with the tenant, you may be tempted to go easy on them and give them more of a chance than perhaps an agent would.

My advice is don't. If they think it's okay to be late paying rent, then they'll keep doing it. The constant hassle for you of chasing them up every month will begin to outweigh the benefit of letting the property, so it would be wise to begin proceedings to evict the tenant and claim the money owing.

How to take action

You don't want your tenant to think you or your letting agent are a soft touch, so it is vital to start proceedings as soon as possible when the rent goes into arrears.

If you have a tenancy agreement in place your tenant should be paying at least a month in advance and you need to stick to this agreement, otherwise you can end up with all sorts of problems, i.e. the tenant might think they can miss a month while they're waiting for their wages to come in, or they promise to pay double in the future.

Experience has taught me that the moment you start feeling sorry for your tenant and accept their reasons for needing more time to pay, the more likely you are to end up out of pocket. There will be genuine cases, however most of the time it eventually becomes clear that delayed payments are simply an attempt at avoiding paying altogether.

So when should you start taking action on your bad tenant?

- A day or two late. There is no harm in making a phone call to ask what's happening with the rent, if only to make sure that everything is ok.

- A week late. You or your letting agent should already be sending the tenant a polite letter reminding them that the rent is overdue. At this stage it could be an oversight and you don't want to accuse or antagonise your tenant.

- Two weeks late. By now the tenant has had plenty of time to pay. They may come back with excuses, but now is the time for you to appoint a solicitor or eviction specialist to begin the process of recovering the rent arrears.

TIP: *Act quickly!*

The longer you or your agent delays the process of taking action on late payment, the longer you'll be waiting for your cash. If you're relying on the income you make from rent, this can be a big problem for you.

What to do if your tenant is damaging your property

Rent arrears are one thing, damaging your property is another and if the damage is caused by carelessness or neglect, you should act swiftly to recover the cost of the repair.

Some people will advise you to simply deduct the money from the tenant's deposit but if they stay in the property and continue to cause damage, the repair costs can soon stack up until you end up with a shortfall.

It's far better to insist that they pay up immediately for any damage, rather than have them sitting in the property for another two months, possibly causing more. (I say two months because that's the minimum notice a landlord must give the tenant on an assured shorthold tenancy agreement.)

How to get rid of a bad tenant

Getting rid of your tenant isn't as easy as simply kicking them out when things go wrong or sending in the heavies! The law in this country protects tenants very well and they have the right to be left to live in peace in your property. Anything you do that appears remotely threatening can leave you in hot water, rather than the tenant, regardless of whether they owe you rent or have caused upset or damage.

So when you decide enough is enough and you want to get rid of a troublesome tenant, you need to act not only with speed but with clear knowledge of how the law works.

If you want to evict a tenant before the agreement is up, you will need to go to court. You must make sure that all your paperwork is in order and you have followed the correct procedures, issuing notices in the right order and at the right time.

Two months is the minimum period you need in most cases and it can take a month or so for the case to go to court – then you will need to wait for the court to order the tenant to vacate the property.

The most common reasons for evicting a tenant are rent arrears, persistent late payment of rent, damage to the property and antisocial behaviour.

In most cases you will need a Section 21 notice. It is worth checking with your agent or an eviction specialist, or even websites such as Shelter, to see the latest rules regarding particular types of tenancy agreements, because advice will be pro-tenant and there may be some loopholes you hadn't thought about.

For your Section 21 notice to be valid, it needs to be in writing and give the tenant two months to leave and it **must** be served in the correct manner. After this notice period expires, the court can evict a tenant at any time. If you have a change of heart and decide to let your tenant stay, then they misbehave again and you want to evict them, you will need to issue another notice as the first one will no longer be valid.

For more information on the rights of tenants visit england.shelter. org.uk

Putting up the rent

Raising rents can mean a mixture of pleasure and pain for the typical buy to let landlord. Naturally you don't want to upset your loyal tenant by raising their rent but, at the same time, knowing you can increase your profits every now and then simply by charging someone more for the accommodation you're providing is one of the many perks of investing in property.

That doesn't mean you can simply put the rent up whenever you like. If the rental period is fixed for six or 12 months, then you can't increase the rent during this period - unless you insert a clause that allows for it.

You may want to do that, but amending tenancy agreements in this way is likely to result in your tenants viewing you as a bit of a chancer who's going to take advantage of them, and they'll simply go and rent somewhere else instead. The most reasonable thing for you to do is set the rent according to local market comparables and at a rate you're comfortable with.

Most landlords will let property on a six or 12-month term, therefore it won't be long before you can either raise the rent or find a new tenant willing to pay it.

TIP: *Don't be too greedy with rent.*

Be careful if you intend to raise the rent to a level that might be seen as unreasonable by the tenant. It could result in the tenant delaying payment while they appeal against the increase. They're unlikely to pay if the amount is in dispute because doing so would be regarded as acceptance of the increase. Being too greedy could put a dent in your cash flow and lose you a tenant.

Real life example:

A penthouse owner decided to let his apartment for £1200 a month in an area where there wasn't a great deal of demand for properties of that type. Even so, he managed to find a tenant willing to pay the high monthly rent. The tenant moved in and things went well until the owner decided to pass on a large chunk of his monthly service charge to the tenant.

The tenant moved out due to the landlord failing to disclose the extra costs up front and the property remained empty for several months. You will get far more respect from your tenants if you're transparent and clear about the amount they will be expected to pay. Losing a tenant over technicalities is a false economy.

How to prepare for when a tenancy comes to an end

Long-term tenants are nice to have and some can be with you for years but the average rental period for someone on an Assured Shorthold Tenancy is around nine months.

This nine months can whizz by quickly. Ending a tenancy comes with its own set of tasks for landlords or estate agents as it involves administration, inspection of the property, calculating how much of the deposit you need to retain to cover cleaning and (or) repairs, and then carrying out any maintenance in preparation for the new tenant.

You will also need to set aside time to make sure you market the property well in advance of the current tenant moving out and have a new one lined up to move in, so you don't suffer any void periods.

Check for damage and wear and tear

You should arrange a visit to your tenant's property a week or two before they move out so that you have time to assess how much work needs to be done to tidy up the property and obtain quotes, if there's anything you feel the tenant should pay for.

If there is wear and tear and you're confident that you can prove any damage is as a direct result of the tenant's neglect or lack of care, then you should be able to deduct the cost from their deposit. If there is a dispute over whether the tenant is liable for any damage, cleaning costs, replacement of items, etc., then you will need to approach the tenancy deposit scheme provider where you lodged their deposit. They will mediate and make a ruling.

TIP: *Keep all furniture, fixtures and fittings receipts and note all communications*

This will help date and value the items in your property, so that if there is a dispute over damage, you have evidence to support the cost of replacement or repair. Also make sure you keep clear records of when damage was noticed, reported and brought to the tenant's attention, and copies of any letters you sent asking them to pay for it.

Things to do to prepare for the next tenant

- Make sure your current tenant(s) vacates the property on time.
- Ask the tenant to leave the property in good order. Having them clean the property can save you a lot of work.
- If there are carpets, make sure you or the tenant gets them professionally cleaned. (If they were professionally cleaned when the tenant moved in, they should pay for the same to be done when they move out.)

- ○ Make sure the kitchen is clean. Dirty ovens and broken kitchen units can put prospective tenants off or reduce the amount of rent they're willing to pay.
- ○ Fling open the windows and install some air fresheners. There's nothing worse than a property that still smells of its previous owners!

Chapter 11

A Landlord's Responsibilities

Becoming a landlord places all kinds of demands on you. The more properties you accumulate, the more these responsibilities grow and you'll need to exercise good judgement in a variety of areas to be successful. Some responsibilities you can delegate while others will require more of your personal input.

Your legal responsibilities as a landlord

It is your responsibility to ensure that the property you are letting is safe for your tenant and maintained to a decent standard.

We hear far less about neglectful landlords these days than was once the case. There used to be a lot of stories on the news about 'rogue' landlords who were careless with gas boilers or gas fires before safety checks and certification were a legal requirement.

A lot of legislation has now been brought in to protect tenants from careless landlords. Your letting agent will be able to provide you with a list of everything you should be aware of and all the checks that need to be carried out before you can safely let your property.

The following are of particular importance:

Key areas	Responsibilities
Gas safety	Equipment must be safely installed by a Gas Safe engineer. You must give a copy of the safety certificate to the tenant and carry out checks annually.
Electrical safety	A 'Part P' registered electrician should check that all electrical fittings and appliances are safe.
Fire safety	Provide fire alarms and extinguishers and if providing furniture, make sure it's fire safe.
Maintenance	You will be responsible for repairs to the property.

In addition to the above areas related to the inside of the property, if there is a garden, garage or other outbuilding, you may be responsible for some maintenance, depending on your agreement with the tenant.

Protecting your tenant's deposit

Since April 2007, it has been a legal requirement for all tenant deposits to be protected in one of the Government's approved schemes. The deposit can't be treated as some extra cash to spend or used to help cash flow during the tenancy.

The reason this was introduced was to protect tenants against unethical landlords making up spurious excuses to keep hold of the whole deposit at the end of the tenancy. Now you need to have a good reason to withhold or deduct any of this deposit when the tenancy agreement comes to an end.

You can legally make reasonable deductions for:

- Damage to the property
- Missing items
- Cleaning
- Unpaid rent

You won't be able to claim for things like wear and tear on carpets, however if someone burns a hole in it, then this would fall under damage, and you should be able to use the deposit money to buy a new one.

If there is any dispute, the tenancy deposit scheme provider will ask both you and the tenant to put forward your cases to them, along with all supporting evidence. They may also visit the property themselves. Their decision is final and the authorised amount will be returned to each party – or the whole deposit to one party, if that is their conclusion.

Why you shouldn't 'bother' your tenants

You may have already concluded that the less 'hands on' you are, the better time you will have in buy to let investing. This includes keeping your relationship with tenants professional.

The last thing a tenant needs is for you to be popping round every couple of weeks checking on things. Tenants like to make a place a home even if they're only staying for a few months. And it's important for you to remember that your tenants have a legal right to 'peaceful enjoyment' of the property while they live there.

Tenants have been known to change the locks to stop the landlord entering the property when they're not around. Being locked out of a property you own is not ideal, so make the tenant aware in the tenancy agreement of how much notice you will give them for a visit.

It's a crime to withhold your details from the tenant

As much as you might want to check on your tenant and contact them, they have a similar right and are legally entitled to know your name and your UK contact address. Either you or your letting agent needs to give them this information and if you refuse you can be prosecuted, so be warned.

Chapter 12

Tax And Property Investment

The most onerous side of property investment is calculating your tax liability and it certainly pays to have an accountant who is familiar with buy to let portfolios, to help you pay as little tax as possible on your buy to let income.

I'm not going to tell you ways to avoid paying tax or advise you on your tax affairs (a) because I'm not qualified to do so and (b) because everyone's tax affairs are different.

There are ways to keep tax down, but if you don't pay what you owe, you will end up with a fine or a court appearance and could possibly even face jail time for tax avoidance.

Entire books are written on tax and property investment but for the purposes of this one, I'll simply give you an outline of your liabilities as a buy to let investor and ways it is possible to offset the amount the HMRC will inevitably take away.

Information on tax can, of course, change with each passing Budget. At the time of writing, buy to let investors are firmly on the radar of the HMRC, particularly when it comes to holiday rentals.

Powerful lobby groups are also putting pressure on the Government to end some of the tax advantages that have resulted in an explosion in the popularity of buy to let over the past couple of decades.

According to data reported in the Telegraph newspaper in 2013, landlords claimed £13bn in allowable expenses to offset against rent. This is said to have taken between £3bn and £5bn from the Government's coffers which, historically, is something that doesn't go down too well with the administration.

A lot of people think that landlords are responsible for things like unsustainable house price inflation and that it's all down to the tax relief landlords get. A lobby group called PricedOut discovered that 17% of sitting MPs were landlords, compared with just 4% of the population as a whole, and argued that they therefore had a clear incentive to keep the status quo!

So if we assume that nothing will change too much in the next few years, there are four ways the tax man can take money from you:

Capital Gains Tax

Capital gains tax (CGT) is what you may need to pay if you sell your investment property for a profit. You won't be asked to pay this tax if you make a loss and sometimes you may even be able to reduce your CGT liability by including some of the expenses you will have incurred in letting and preparing a property for rent.

As of 2014/15 you automatically get a tax-free allowance of £11,000 on the gains you make through the course of the tax year. If you decide to sell your investment property you should declare that you have done so on your self-assessment tax return.

Capital gains is charged at either 18% or 28%, depending on the amount of capital gain you have made in the tax year. Some of the expenses you can deduct from your capital gain include:

- Estate/letting agent fees
- Solicitor's fees
- Costs of advertising the property for sale
- Stamp Duty
- Refurbishment costs (but not general maintenance)

Stamp Duty Land Tax

Stamp Duty is one of those areas the Government likes to play with. It is the tax you pay when you buy any property in the UK costing £125,001 or more.

£0 - £125,000	0%
£125,001 - £250,000	1%
£250,001 - £500,000	3%
£500,001 - £1,000,000	4%
£1,000,001 - £2,000,000	5%
Over £2,000,000	7%

The same stamp duty rate is payable whether you are a buy to let investor or a homebuyer.

If you're buying some of the cheaper housing in cities in the North of the UK, you can save yourself paying this tax if you buy below the £125,001 threshold.

Income Tax

If you're generating an income from renting out a property, you will of course be liable to pay some income tax on it. As with all tax liabilities, if you don't declare the money you're making you may get a penalty from the tax office.

According to current income tax rules, you must report any income you make in the tax year over £2,500 on your Self-Assessment tax return.

If it's less than £2,500 a year, the advice is to ring the Self-Assessment Helpline and ask for a P810 form.

The good news with income tax is, you can claim a lot of costs and offset them against your income to lower your tax bill. There are different rules for the following:

- Residential properties
- Furnished holiday lettings

What you can claim for

Residential Property	Furnished Holiday Lettings*
Letting agents fees	10% of net rent as a 'wear and tear allowance'
Legal fees for lets of one year or less	Plant machinery and capital allowances
Accountancy fees	Equipment used outside the property such as vans and tools
Buildings and contents insurance	Capital gains tax relief
Interest on property loans	
Maintenance and repairs	
Utility bills	
Rent, ground rent, service charges	
Council tax	
Cleaning/ gardening	
Direct letting costs e.g. advertising	

Inheritance Tax (IHT)

A lot of people decide to get into buy to let investing not only to make money but also to leave something behind for their families. So if you're planning to leave your family some cash behind and make sure they get to see the benefit of the work you're putting into property investment, then you need to plan ahead.

Inheritance tax is what the government takes from your estate after you die and they will assess your entire estate so that they can redistribute a large percentage of the wealth you have accumulated during your lifetime.

If you don't have very much, then IHT won't be a concern, but I assume that as you're reading this book you will already be planning to make a million or more from property investment.

If you're already making a million, then you will be over the current threshold, which stands at £325,000. Anything over this threshold is taxable at 40%. It does seem unfair, considering that you have already paid your fair share of tax, only to have the Government take another big chunk away when you're gone, but that's just the way it is.

IHT calculation example:

> Julian leaves his children a portfolio of properties worth £800,000.

His children will not see anything taken away on the first £325,000. Unfortunately, the remaining £475,000 will be liable for 40% tax.

Julian's family lose £190,000 of their inheritance to IHT.

But things are rarely this straightforward when it comes to inheritance:

If Julian is married and has no children, his wife is not required to pay any inheritance tax on the £800,000 he leaves behind.

If, on the other hand, Julian is married with children then things get a little more complicated – or a little more interesting, depending on how you view it.

Julian dies with a portfolio of properties worth £800,000. He leaves £200,000 of the value of his estate to his children in his Will.

Because he didn't use up the full tax-free allowance of £325,000, the remaining £125,000 passes on to his wife and her allowance is increased to £450,000

Eventually, when she passes away with assets of £600,000, 40% IHT will be due on anything over the £450,000.

40% of £150,000 is £60,000, leaving the children with £540,000.

By leaving the full £800,000 to his children in his Will, the family lost £190,000 to IHT, but by splitting his estate, they only lost £60,000. So, rather than £610,000 inheritance, the children would have £740,000, saving £130,000 from disappearing into Government coffers.

As you can see, it's well worth speaking to a solicitor and an accountant to find the best way for you to pass on your wealth.

But what if I'm not married?
If you're not married or in a civil partnership, then the above tax breaks don't apply and inheritance tax will need to be paid on anything over the £325,000 threshold.

How else can I reduce IHT liability?
One way to reduce IHT is to gift part of your buy to let property or portfolio as an undivided share to another member of your family. You will need to survive for seven years for this to take effect but,

even if you leave it late, three years will be enough to see some reduction in what your estate is liable to pay.

The biggest single thing you can do to reduce inheritance tax is to make a Will and get an expert to advise you on all the various tax issues. This may cost a bit of money, but spending a few thousand on advice can save the ones you leave behind hundreds of thousands of pounds.

Congratulations!

By buying, reading and getting this far through my book you are clearly destined for success in property investment.

Visit the **free resources** section of nickfox.co.uk, where you can download further useful tools and resources, plus access excerpts from my other books.

PART FOUR:
CONSOLIDATION

Chapter 13

Portfolio Building

Building a portfolio of buy to let properties is where the returns start to get really interesting, but you do need cash to achieve this. There is no such thing as a 'no money down' deal any more so you need to be prepared and able to borrow or fund the purchase of more properties using the income from your day job or the profit you generate from your other properties.

You could fund purchases through re-mortgaging and releasing capital, depending on how much equity you have in your existing properties and how willing the banks are to lend you money for a buy to let mortgage.

Let's say you manage to raise £100,000 or you receive it as a pension lump sum. What do you do? Is it enough to invest?

Even if you do invest it, it sounds like a lot of money to lose, doesn't it? This is until you see what happens when you build a portfolio.

The important thing to appreciate – and it's one of the most fundamental reasons why property is such an incredible investment vehicle – is just how far that £100,000 can be stretched.

One of the worst-kept secrets in property investment is that the more you stretch the money you have, the more money you can make in property and here's why.

If you invest all that cash in one property that costs you £100,000 and the market is growing at 5% a year, you could sell that property and make £5,000.

If, once you buy that property, you rent it out for £750 a month and your costs are, say £100 a month, then you will be left with £7,800 a year to add to that £5,000 capital increase. Do bear in mind, though, that you will have tax to pay on your income and on the profits from any sale.

If you keep the property long term and don't sell, then your rent will rise steadily but your return on capital will be making less than a 2.5% return on your property unless you put the rent up in year two.

Now let's consider how leveraging using the bank's money and buying more than one property can make a big difference to your bottom line.

With £100,000 cash at your disposal, the bank should be in a position to give you more than one buy to let mortgage, so you can start building a portfolio of properties by leveraging your money, instead of spending it all on one property.

If we assume that the LTV is a conservative 75% then buying three properties with a mortgage will use up £75,000 of your money. You still have the remaining £25,000 to cover your costs and expenses.

You now have three investment properties worth £300,000 in total. If each of the three investment properties rises in value by 5% a year, then instead of getting a 5% return on your whole £100,000, you're getting a 20% return on your investment of £75,000. You've made an extra £10,000 and still have £25,000 in the bank!

So you've made £15,000 in a year on the value of the portfolio alone. You could decide to sell the properties and realise a little bit of profit, but the smart property investors don't sell their properties – they use them for ongoing income.

The actual income you make while you're building your portfolio will come from the rent your tenants pay. So, looking at your investment: the bank invests the lion's share of money in your portfolio, while the tenant gives you the income you need to continue investing in more properties. Now you're starting to make Other People's Money work for you!

The trick is to make sure that the properties you're investing in are available at or below market value and local rents will cover your mortgage payments and any bills, so that at no point do you have to subsidise the investment.

The mortgage costs of running 3 properties valued at £100,000 will be around £18,000 or £1500 a month.

If you can let all three properties for £750 a month then your rental income will be £2,250 a month.

This leaves you with £750 a month or £9,000 a year before any costs are deducted. (Remember, you can offset some of your tax liability against the running costs of each of your properties.)

If we assume that you stop at three properties and the price you originally paid doubles in 10 years, then you will hold three assets worth a total of £600,000. Now you can see, the bigger your portfolio the more money you can make. The only real hurdle you face is getting finance to make this possible.

There are some people who tell you that putting in a larger deposit is better because you will have more equity. If it's your own home, on which you have to pay the mortgage out of your own earnings, it might make you feel more secure to have an equity 'cushion'. But in buy to let, as long as the portfolio is comfortably covering its own running costs and turning a good profit, the LTV doesn't really matter.

When you're investing in property, you need to keep as much of your cash as possible available to reinvest. The less money you have tied up, the more possibilities you have to eventually build that million pound property portfolio!

Spreading your risk

How successful you are at building a property portfolio depends on how much you spread your risk. You could quite happily invest in UK property and spread your risk with different types of property investment in different towns and cities.

Some investors might be tempted by the enticing returns to be found in more exotic locations around the world. Spreading risk, however, shouldn't be about taking uncalculated ones in markets you don't know a lot about. Investing in one bad property or losing money in an investment that turns out to be too good to be true can easily wipe out other profits and have a negative impact on your ability to grow your portfolio.

In property investment it's better to be the tortoise than the hare. You need to generate returns smartly over time, rather than get carried away by clever headlines in property brochures promising amazing returns.

If, on the other hand, you really want to go for it and you're certain that you can absorb any losses from investing in high growth markets, then this is a strategy that can certainly generate wealth faster than investing in the UK – if you get involved early enough in the market growth cycle and things go according to plan.

Property experts used to recommend dividing your property portfolio as follows:

> 60% in safe markets
> 30% in high-growth markets
> 10% in speculative markets

The financial crisis changed this way of thinking. There are fewer high-growth markets left in the world after the great global property boom burnt itself out in 2008. There are still some opportunities in emerging markets, but emerging market investing is far more risky now than it was 10 years ago.

Property bubbles are commonplace and as recovery returns to more familiar markets like the UK, France, Germany and so on, it's wiser to look closer to home if you want to take a risk.

What are the risks of investing in UK property?

	Low Risk	Medium Risk	High Risk	
Property prices falling	√			The UK is at the beginning of a new growth cycle
Risk of a property 'bubble'		√		Outside London this is unlikely. Mortgage lending remains tight
Risk of oversupply		√		Oversupply is an issue in some parts of the UK but not in and around London and the South East
Oversupply of rental properties	√			Rental demand remains high in most part of the UK
Falling property sales		√		Property sales are set to be affected by tighter rules on mortgages

A lot of the above will depend on the area you decide to invest in but, as a rule of thumb, this can be applied to any property market and if you're investing abroad you might also add currency fluctuations into this table.

Turkey, for example, saw a dramatic decline in the value of its currency against Sterling and the Dollar in early 2014. This effectively meant that property bought in Turkey was cheaper in currency terms.

An example of spreading risk within the UK might be to invest in a diverse portfolio of residential properties, from high-yielding HMOS to student lets and family homes.

How to insulate yourself from housing market bubbles and crashes

We've already established that property markets move in cycles, so another crash (or adjustment) is inevitable in the future. Many people were fooled into thinking that property prices would rise forever in the heady days of 2005, until market forces once again conspired to end one of the biggest property booms in history.

So how do you insulate your portfolio from the worst that a downturn can throw at you?

The best way to insulate yourself against a future property market crash is to plan to hold your property long term. If you take the short-term view, you will always run the risk of getting caught out by future property market fluctuations.

"You don't know who's swimming naked until the tide goes out."

In this quote, the world's greatest investor, Warren Buffett, was referring to the business side of investing but it applies equally to property investment too. If you think of the water as your liquidity then if you don't have enough liquidity - i.e. cash flow - to see you through market downturns, the results can be catastrophic not only for your portfolio, but also for your future as an investor.

So insulating yourself from a future crash is about bringing in a level of income that will not be disrupted by what the market happens to be doing. If you can maintain your rental income and it covers your costs from the beginning then you will have nothing to worry about.

If, on the other hand, you take risks with negative cash flow or you buy properties in the hope that they will rise in value by 10% or more, you will get caught out sooner or later.

Property investing is a long-term game, it isn't meant to be a gamble. If you do place a bet on the future you're much more likely to find yourself exposed and swimming naked.

Chapter 14

Your Exit Strategy

An exit strategy is your plan for swapping your asset, which in the case of a buy to let investor is your property or properties, in exchange for some money.

It's all very well having millions of pounds tied up in property, but when the time comes when you want to get out of buy to let, you need to have some kind of strategy in place, and that strategy should be in place from your early days of investing. You should also have some idea of when your exit will be.

People invest and build wealth so that they can 'exit' usually for one or more of the following reasons:

- Property is your pension
- You want to achieve financial freedom
- You want to hand things over to your children

To achieve all of the above, it really comes down to how much money you need and by when. Cash flow generating portfolios are not built overnight. They are built over the course of several years.

A buy and hold strategy should be generating you enough income through rent to make it worthwhile. It's rarely the case that you will make a good rental income when it's easier for people to buy their own property and, likewise, you're unlikely to see high capital growth when property values are falling.

This is why a diverse and balanced portfolio will help you achieve your aims of a retirement income or financial freedom. Nobody can tell you exactly what your exit strategy should be without knowing how much money you need to make from the sale of your properties. In some cases it may be easier just to hang on to them if you have enough income.

If you have invested in the right types of properties, your ownership costs will fall over time. Regular checks on your mortgage rates and the length of time you have left on them will help you set a firm date for your exit.

However, if you have invested in the wrong type of properties, for example, you have too many apartments with hefty service charges that rise every year, then you may be in trouble when it comes to your exit strategy.

If the value of the apartment hasn't increased for several years - and this is the case in many of the UK's apartment-saturated towns and cities - then selling may not be an option. In addition, the income you make from rent will always be affected by things like rising service charges and communal maintenance bills if the block is older.

When property is your pension

Statistics show that one in three people are using property as their pension, to varying degrees. That's a lot of people banking on property to provide them with vital income when they retire.

So how does property stack up against a pension?

If we look at the last decade or so, the story of pensions has not been a happy one. When you put money away into a pension you are essentially giving away control of it to a fund manager who will invest it in a variety of places to generate you a return in the long term.

The idea is that when you retire, you will have a sum of money to maintain your lifestyle. The problem with a pension is that unless you're in a very generous pension scheme that maintains your earnings as in the public sector, you will more than likely be disappointed after collecting your gold clock and waving your work colleagues goodbye.

Have pensions ever lived up to their promises?

They may have done in the past, with the exception of those who got caught out by with Robert Maxwell and Enron.

But the great global downturn of the 2000s changed all that. Suddenly, eye-watering amounts of cash ended up being lost on the stock markets. Annuity rates hit their lowest levels for decades when quantitative easing began to impact on their value.

There was a time at their lowest point in 2012 when £300,000 in our pension pot provided you with an annual income of just £18,000. Not a lot even by today's standards. Now I'm not suggesting that you abandon pensions altogether. It is prudent to diversify your investments for the future to spread your risk. So why not have the best of both worlds?

The last thing you need when you reach retirement is to have to continue working in a menial job to try and make ends meet. Property investment is so popular because it can help you avoid ending up a 'checkout pensioner', working on the tills in a supermarket to make ends meet, and can provide you with a much better standard of living when you're too old to be part of the rat race.

The great thing about becoming a property investor is that you are in control of your investment. As long as the tenant pays the bills and covers all your costs with some left over to generate a profit, then you will be well on the road to generating enough income to sustain your lifestyle in the future.

Summary

Planning for a future where there will be more older people chasing a dwindling amount of state pension payments means that the need has never been greater to plan your financial future.

Becoming a buy to let investor is a positive step towards securing that financial future. The only surprise is that more people are not doing it. Not everyone has the means or the cash to begin, but if you do, then investing in the right property in the right location is one of the safest investments you can make.

Best of all, property is a tangible investment, something secure that you can fall back on in an increasingly virtual world where nothing is certain and the gap between rich and poor is rising.

If you own a property portfolio, you will be able to insulate yourself from the worst that economic downturns can throw at you because:

Property is an appreciating asset. It is virtually guaranteed to grow in value over time.

Your tenants will cover the cost of ownership and generate a profit for you.

You can borrow and leverage the bank's money to buy more properties that will increase your profits dramatically.

Compared to other investments, such as the stock market, you will not be risking 100% of your money. This simply can't happen with property. Yes there will be downturns and economic cycles, but in the long term, property anywhere will rise in value simply with inflation.

People talk of buying property as 'getting on the ladder'. I like to think of it as getting on an escalator because your investment rises the longer you hold on to it.

Long term, property prices only tend to ever go in one direction and that's up.

The number of properties you can own when you step onto our theoretical escalator is only limited by three things: time, energy and resources. If you can manage all three then you will be well on the way to financial freedom!

I wish you the best of luck on your journey!

Nick

Even more...
...from Nick Fox Property Mentoring.

Thank you for taking the time to read our book; we hope you've found it helpful. If you'd like to extend your knowledge, please check out our website, where you'll find a wealth of free information and details of our mentoring packages.

We offer a range of mentoring options to suit all needs, from short intensive taster sessions to more comprehensive packages that will give you a deeper understanding of property investment and the buy to let market, focusing on the rewards and implications of building an HMO portfolio.

Various choices available include:

- Half-day 'HMO Education and Tour'
- One-day 'Intensive HMO Property Mentoring Course'
- Two-day 'Intensive HMO Property Mentoring Course'
- 12 months' full access to and support from Nick Fox and his Power Team

Whichever package you choose, you can be assured that Nick's commitment to your personal property goals are absolute. Nick and his team get a real kick out of watching others grow their property portfolios by helping them implement the most successful methods that have been tried and tested over many years.

As skilled and experienced professionals, we present our mentoring sessions in such a way that they are easy to understand, while enabling highly effective learning. The acute insights and practical methodology on offer will help you to take your property business to the next level and secure financial independence for you and your loved ones.

Check out our website **www.nickfox.co.uk** or call us on **01908 930369** to find out more.

Find us on FACEBOOK Nick Fox Mentor TWITTER @foxytowers
www.nickfox.co.uk EMAIL hello@nickfox.co.uk TEL 01908 930369
NICK FOX PROPERTY MENTORING
14 Wharfside Bletchley Milton Keynes MK2 2AZ

nickfox
property mentoring

Read on...

Collect the set of books by Nick Fox to help you achieve financial freedom through property investment.

HMO PROPERTY SUCCESS

Do you want a secure financial future that starts sooner, rather than later as you're approaching retirement? By investing in multi-let properties, you can double or even triple the level of rental income generated by single letting, and realise positive cash flow from the start. In this book, multiple business owner and investor, Nick Fox, clearly guides you through the steps to building an HMO portfolio that delivers both on-going income and a tangible pension or lifestyle pot.

ISBN: 978-0-9576516-0-9
RRP: £9.99

PROPERTY INVESTMENT SUCCESS

How does your financial future look?
If you haven't reviewed your pension provision for a while or aren't completely happy with how your current investments are performing, you should take a closer look at property. In this book, Nick Fox discusses the pros and cons of traditional pensions and makes the case for property as a robust alternative investment vehicle.
He looks at how property can deliver different kinds of returns at different times and shows how you can build a tailored portfolio that perfectly satisfies your own future financial needs.

ISBN: 978-0-9576516-4-7
RRP: £9.99

FIRST TIME PROPERTY DEVELOPER

Interested in developing property for profit ? Don't know where
to start? Let experienced property expert, Nick Fox, lead
you through the process. Nick will show you how to find the
property, add genuine value to it by developing and refurbishing
and then explain how to sell on for profit or rent out for income.

ISBN: 978-0-9576516-4-7
RRP: £9.99

101 TOP TIPS FOR PROPERT INVESTMENT SUCCESS

Whether you're looking to focus purely on HMOs, build a varied
portfolio of rental properties, or employ a number of different
strategies to make money from property, '101 TOP TIPS' is full
of useful information that will help keep you at the top of the
property investment business.
Nick Fox has spent the past decade amassing a highly
profitable buy to let portfolio and continues to invest in a
variety of property projects and business ventures. His tailored
mentoring programmes have helped many aspiring investors
realise their own potential in the property field.

ISBN: 978-0-9935074-9-6 | RRP: £9.99

PROPERTY RENNOVATION & REFURBISHMENT SUCCESS

Successful renovation and refurbishment relies on spending
the right amount of money in the right way, so are you ready to
hone your budgeting, planning and project-management skills?
Alongside the deposit, this is where the biggest chunk of your
investment funds will be spent. You need to analyse the figures,
budget correctly, plan the work in detail and ensure it's carried
out properly so that your buy to let performs as you need it to.
Not sure how to do that? Then this is the book for you!

ISBN: 978-0-9927817-6-7
RRP: £11.99

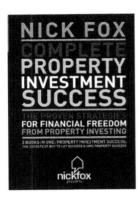

COMPLETE PROPERTY INVESTMENT SUCCESS

This indispensable trilogy takes you through the pros and cons of property as an investment vehicle, looks at the business of buy to let and the different ways you can make money from property, then goes into detail about how to successfully source, refurbish and let out highly cash-positive houses in multiple occupation.

ISBN: 978-0-9927817-0-5
RRP: £26.99

COMPLETE HMO PROPERTY SUCCESS

This HMO 'superbook' is essential reading for anyone who's starting out in property investment and wants to generate income.

It begins by looking at investing in Houses in Multiple Occupation as a business and takes you through how to successfully source, refurbish, let out and manage a highly cash-positive portfolio.

The second part then focuses on the all-important renovation stage. It details how to budget, plan your works, manage your project and carry out the refurbishment in such a way that your HMO performs as you need it to and you get the returns you're looking for.

A prolific and highly successful investor, Nick's personal portfolio extends to more than 200 properties, both shared accommodation and single household lets – and he also has interests in several development projects around the UK.

ISBN: 978-0-9935074-0-3 | RRP: £19.99

Available now online at
www.amazon.co.uk & www.nickfox.co.uk
Books, iBook, Kindle & Audio

Find us on FACEBOOK Nick Fox Mentor TWITTER NickFoxPropertyMentoring
www.nickfox.co.uk EMAIL hello@nickfox.co.uk TEL 01908 930369
NICK FOX PROPERTY MENTORING
14 Wharfside Bletchley Milton Keynes MK2 2AZ

Amazon reviews for HMO Property Success

'A brilliant book'

What sets Nick Fox' book apart from others is the amount of practical detail and advice. It provides a solid and clean framework and a step-by-step guide on how to find, fund, fill and run a profitable house in multiple occupancy. This book has no fluff – it is a very valuable and easy read.

nc3134, 17 Nov 2013

'A MUST read for any HMO owner or investor'

This book is concise, well written, well informed and very practical. I have many other property books but this is by far the best and a must for anyone wanting to invest in HMO property.

Mark MTC, 23 Jan 2014

'Best Property Investment Book'

This no-nonsense approach will guide anyone who is interested in the HMO market into a successful investment; unlike many other publications that purport to be able to help people "get

rich quick" with "no money down"; this insightful guide is realistic and proven.
RegSupport, 17 Nov 2013

'Step by step guide to HMO investing'
It is rare in a property book of this kind to find so much solid advice and what must have been hard-earned knowledge - in comparison most other books on the subject provide next to no real information on how to get started. Everyone thinking of getting into hmo property investing should buy this book!
AndyP, 1 Dec 2013

'Great book – especially for those looking to start building a HMO portfolio'
I'm not new to property but am about to start building a HMO portfolio and this book gave me some excellent advice not available in other publications. It also gave me the confidence to proceed down the HMO route!
Stephen Whall, 28 March 2014

Using an easy to understand and simple format, this book is highly effective and informative, neither superficial nor "salesy". A pleasant read for anyone who is time poor and wants to learn HMO property investing.
K Devos, 9 Jan 2014

'Excellent Book'

There are no hard sells, no "get rich" quickly advice, it simply tells you that Nick's investment strategy has proven to give successful results. I strongly advise you to read this book if you are serious about investing.

Elda Breuer, 5 Feb 2014

Testimonials

"I met Nick back in 2013, having been referred through a mutual friend. We hit it off from day one! Nick took me through and explained his entire business: how he had built it up over the years, the ups and downs, and how he had fine-tuned systems and processes to ensure his portfolio and tenants were well managed and producing the correct level of financial return.

I already had a portfolio and a considerable amount of experience in property, having built a substantial letting agency through the 1990s and a property maintenance business in 2003, nevertheless, Nick was still able teach me a great deal.

I was impressed with Nick's openness and honesty. He has very deep knowledge and is without doubt a leading expert in the buy to let property field. Mentor - now business partner and friend."
Richard Leonard, Herts

"Nick and his team are the real deal. Their knowledge and help in moving my investment project forward has been invaluable. Without their expertise I would not have been able to reach my personal property goals or milestones."
Richard Felton, UK

"Nick is a very experienced property professional. His practical advice on setting goals, the pros and cons of this type of investment and how to minimise risks and properly manage a growing portfolio are essential in what can be a very complex investment.

Nick's mentoring is not a get-rich-quick formula but a clear and concise way of demonstrating how a solid property investment strategy can be put into action. And the results are well worth it."
D.Wright, Aberdeen

"Great book, great guy and great results for me after I read 'HMO Property Success'. I've now replaced my job with passive income from HMO properties. Thanks, Nick!"
C.Clark, Bedford

"Nick has clearly got a huge amount of knowledge in his field, and having his support and experience has given me the increased confidence to make my first steps into investing."
Craig Smith, Edinburgh

"I have spent money in the past on various property courses, where you are taught in a group in a classroom, and those have not really helped me. This one-to-one mentoring with Nick was brilliant, as I was actually seeing his business and properties, meeting tenants, getting lots of advice and seeing what worked well and what didn't in a live situation. I have booked another two days

with Nick in my home city next week, to look at various properties and hopefully start my journey as a full-time property investor, and I cannot wait! I highly recommend this type of mentoring!"
James Robinson, Hull

"Both Sarah and I cannot express how much help Nick has been to our property business over the last two years. His support and knowledge have been invaluable. We would thoroughly recommend his mentoring to any budding investor."
Stuart Lewis, Northampton

"Thank you so much for your patience, professionalism and general understanding during our three-day mentoring programme. The visit to see how your office and HMO business runs was incredible and so, so helpful. Without it we would have been at a complete loss. With your guidance and help we have now purchased our first HMO property and look forward to keeping in touch to show you our profitable progress!"
Rebecca Santay-Jones, Harrow

Lightning Source UK Ltd.
Milton Keynes UK
UKOW05f0607190417
299439UK00016B/412/P